WOMEN WHO TALK TO THE DEAD

WOMEN WHO TALK TO THE DEAD

The True Story of 200 Forgotten Murder Victims and the Relentless Pursuit of Justice by an FBI Agent and a Detroit Police Detective

KATHERINE SCHWEIT

Cover photos provided by and used with permission from the Federal Bureau of Investigation.

ISBN 978-1-947635-79-1
Library of Congress Control Number: 2025905456
Published by 82 Stories

To learn more, please visit KatherineSchweit.com.

Dedication

That the unnamed are found.

Introduction

This is the extraordinary true story of women who speak to the dead. Not through séances or spiritualism, but through science, determination, and an unwavering commitment to give names back to Detroit's forgotten murder victims.

For over half a century, hundreds of people were buried anonymously in pauper graves across Detroit's outskirts—victims of homicide whose identities remained unknown, their murders unsolved. They were buried in rows, sometimes stacked three deep in concrete vaults, their only markers a series of numbers in fading cemetery logs. Each was someone's child, parent, sibling, or friend. Each had a name before they became just another cold case file gathering dust in a converted grocery warehouse.

Follow the remarkable five-year journey of an unlikely team of female investigators who pledged to identify and resolve over 200 of Detroit's outstanding murder cases where the unidentified were buried in paupers' graves. Led by Detroit Police Detective Shannon Jones and FBI Special Agent Leslie Larsen, this group of dedicated women—detectives, agents, forensic anthropologists, and scientists—literally dug through the past to bring closure to families and justice to the murdered.

Their quest would become Operation UNITED, the largest coordinated exhumation of unidentified murder victims in FBI history. Through rain and mud, facing bureaucratic hurdles and limited resources, these women meticulously unearthed and documented remains, collected DNA samples, and piece by piece, began solving decades-old homicides that many had long forgotten.

This is not just a story of innovative forensic techniques or cold case investigation. It's an intimate look at the investigators who refused to let these murders go unsolved and to leave the families behind in the wake of violence. When a murdered person is buried anonymously, they leave behind a gaping hole in the fabric of their family—a wound that can only begin to heal when the truth is finally revealed.

Even today, investigators need the public's help to provide information and potential DNA matches to identify these unknown victims and help solve the murders. These women embody the promise to "never forget" in their quest to bring families back together and, in the process, close Detroit's outstanding cold case murder files permanently. Their story reminds us that long after the news stories end and public attention fades, dedicated investigators remain committed to speaking for those who can no longer speak for themselves.

Contents

CHAPTER 1

The Lady Vanishes

"Can I stay at my cousin's tonight?" asks the just 14-year-old as his mom dresses to go out. It is 1987. *He sits on her bed, watching as she slips on a pair of red pumps with a red leather bow on the back of each heel. She just has a moment to give him a hug, tell him she loves him and plant a kiss goodbye before he is out the door of their apartment. "Remember," she tells him, "We all we got."*

The words are hard earned. She was only 14 when he was born, only a child herself. Three years later, her mother died of cancer, leaving the 17-year-old to care also for her three younger siblings. She turns to selling drugs to survive. By the time the boy has started school, she has clocked her first two drug arrests. Drug selling became drug using. As he navigates school, more and more he is alone while his mother disappears for days at a time.

He loves being home and with her. Therefore, it's upsetting, but not surprising, when he returns from his cousin's place to find an empty house. But he couldn't have known it was the last time. No one could have known. He waited for her, as he always did.

The boy doesn't hear about it, but a few weeks later, Detroit police and firefighters find a home burning on nearby Wanda Street. They discover human remains, including a skull that appeared to have been crushed, perhaps when the top floor caved in or when firefighters were putting out the fire. Nearby, they find the severely burned torso of a woman. She has no identification.

Two handwritten, one-page police reports produced by responding officers, Thomas McFarland and Steven Stewart, use the identical four sentences to explain why they were called to the house by responding fire-fighters. When they first arrive, they observe the body of a female, face up, with legs and arms cut off, but no limbs are found at the scene. They choose to wait outside for homicide detectives. Maybe it is too much to handle. Maybe it is too routine.

Nothing in her lungs indicates she was breathing during the fire, and detectives think she had been strangled to death, most likely before she was brought to the house. The medical examiner determines the cause of death—strangulation. It's homicide. They inventory her meager belongings that will be buried with her: dress, coat, and red shoes with a bow on the back.

She is no longer a neighbor, a worker, or a mom. Now she is a body. The body is loaded into the coroner's truck and driven out of town with other body bags taken from refrigerated storage. Bags and pine boxes are their permanent homes now. A backhoe scrapes off the grass and rich midwestern dirt from the ground. The grave needs to be deep enough to stack three bodies on top of each other. Soon the cemetery workers complete their final act, burying the bodies along with Detroit's many other unidentified homicide victims.

Hours turned into days and days turned to months. The boy is learning how to take care of himself, selling what he can, and clinging with confidence to the knowledge that any moment his mom will return as she always has. He never tells his teachers that his mom is missing. They can tell something is wrong, but no one checks further. Months pass and his 15th birthday arrives. His mother has never missed his birthday, even if it's just a call. In the recesses of his mind, he knows she will not return.

The boy is left to navigate a new world on his own.

CHAPTER 2

Voices Below

"It's DIG DAY," Leslie yells, shaking her wife awake. The first time the exclamation just happened spontaneously, but since then, just as she loved her first day of school as a child, she has been compelled to share her excitement on the first dig of the season.

"IT'S DIG DAY, IT'S DIG DAY," the FBI Special Agent repeats with both hands on Virginia's shoulders, shaking the bed and yelling so loudly she wakes their two kids.

July has arrived. It indeed is time to dig.

Leslie has worked on plenty of exhumations based on court order, but this is a first. Her team will be working alongside the Detroit Police Department to unearth the remains of a few hundred cold case murder victims. Missed evidence or a DNA sample might result in identifying the long-forgotten victim left in a pauper's grave.

With tenacity and a bit of hard work, they will not only reconnect the dead with their families, but their hope is also to solve dozens and dozens of decades-old murders.

Going to the cemetery changes Leslie's focus; everyone's focus. Instead of listening to the voices in the files that they alone seem to be able to hear, they concentrate now on hearing the silent cries or muffled moans of buried murder victims. Leslie's been here before and she knows with 100-percent certainty that if the bones speak, she, and her partner, Detroit Police Detective Shannon Jones, will be able to tell the dig teams where the bones are waiting to be discovered.

They have combed through the files. Now, they need help from the dead who must call up to them. The dig teams will be so close. Just above. To their core, Shannon and Leslie know they must somehow hear the voices to locate the exact locations of the bones, sometimes haphazardly buried, if the upcoming dig week is to be successful.

"I always let the ground talk to me," Leslie admits. "The dead know I'm there to help them. Sometimes they give us hints to help. It's our job to speak for those victims who don't even have a name."

They can't quite explain it, but they have had several discussions about how close they feel to the victims. How they can review a file or be at a scene and envision how their murders occurred. They are one with victims. It's hard to explain. Some say women are more likely to feel the presence of the murder victims underground. Others say the victims are indeed speaking out and only the women are listening. Maybe they are more in tune with the human factor.

Whatever the reason, it is women who make up the overwhelming number of agents, police officers, students, anthropologists, and more who climb from the cars in the cemetery parking lot to dig up the dead year after year.

Some men do get it, Leslie says, but women "have a knack for it."

The two dozen or so murder victims they intend to find today are located west of downtown Detroit in Knollwood Memorial Park Cemetery. The cemetery, in Canton Township, is across from a neighborhood featuring quarter-acre lots, many with oversized houses and wide driveways, basketball hoops, and professionally landscaped yards. A few homes have swimming pools, but for those that don't, residents can use the community pool located just beyond the fence where the digging occurs.

The curious are deterred by the tall, opaque fence and beckoning diving board and kiddie pool. Dig team members appreciate the irony that the neighborhood where they're excavating is filled with nice cars—something that those buried in the paupers' section never owned, but might have dried off at a car wash.

Leslie and Shannon had spent their last free night before a week of digging at the soon-to-be bustling cemetery. All their investigative skills have connected to give them their best estimate for where their target bodies are buried and where to push in the first shovels.

They had walked the cemetery together, looking back and forth at their maps and relying heavily on the cemetery manager and his crew, who have shown up in a grey pickup truck. One by one, they began pounding in 1 x 2-inch wooden stakes and tying pink cards to the top. The tags correspond to case numbers and dig sites and will be the guiding stars for arriving dig teams at daybreak.

"We need to pick up a pallet of water," Leslie says, mostly reminding herself.

At the last minute, FBI Headquarters has reversed field and found the money Leslie needs so team members have been able to fly or drive in and settle down for a good meal and a government-paid-for hotel stay. Leslie asks her team members to arrive by 7:00 a.m. She wants briefings finished, supplies out, and personal protective equipment (PPE) taped to everybody's wrists and ankles by 9:00 a.m. Park in the designated parking area at the far end of the cemetery, their final directions say. And no one better show up at the briefing site until they have reported to the check-in tent down at the end of the road.

Knollwood and another cemetery, United Memorial, have hundreds of paupers' graves. They are about five miles apart as the crow flies and how many bodies Leslie and Shannon will eventually dig up and identify is a bit of a crap shoot right now.

"Shannon isn't sure of the number of cold case murders," Leslie admits. She's still working through the old files. It's somewhere between 258 and 304. Maybe 75 are at Knollwood, but she's not sure how many victims lie below ground at United Memorial.

This morning, crews arriving at Knollwood survey the familiar scene. Beautifully landscaped and flat, the land is covered with blankets of uninterrupted grass. There are a few trees and fewer raised headstones, just the occasional three-inch brass disc pounded into the ground like a mile marker on a highway.

"We mentally prepare for Knollwood differently than we do for United Memorial," Leslie says, surveying the plans for the day from a golf cart she has commandeered. She is referring to United Memorial Gardens in Plymouth, where bodies are not buried in vaults.

"At Knollwood, we know that the majority of those bodies are gonna be in concrete vaults—a big, huge concrete square in the ground, and then there are four packs," she adds. "There's a concrete square with a concrete lid; we take the lid off, and then there's four dead guys stacked in a row. We don't know which dead guy is which dead guy. So those are .. I don't wanna say a sure thing, but the mapping and the records at Knollwood are much more intact and accurate than what we face at United Memorial."

Among the many supporting the efforts is Lori Bruski. She has pored over cemetery records and worked with the cemetery crew to make the best estimate of where they should start digging. Lori is from the National Missing and Unidentified Persons System (NAMUS), a government funded organization that collects information from families with missing loved ones. Both digging successes and failures from the previous year have provided some underground road maps, albeit crude. In some spots, Leslie's team of diggers have left global positioning geomarkers where they dug to help Lori decipher the cemetery below ground.

Shannon is a lone ranger, but she knows everyone in Detroit and knows how to get everything she needs. "I made sure who I had on board and explained what would be required," she tells Leslie. "If there were any funds, we don't want to pay for anything other than the manpower hours. The rest is all donated. I had all the other people donating their personnel. State police donated personnel. The FBI donated personnel."

The Detroit Department of Public Works has provided excavators in the past. On this dig there are skilled utility personnel helping maneuver excavators. "It's a lot of outreaching to the different resources that the city of Detroit has that allowed us to do it," Shannon says. "Everything that I've been working on has all been established through relationships," and then she adds, "right?"

It's a sentence ender Shannon often uses to ensure those around her listen, agree, and don't ask her any follow-up questions. Her judicious use of words matches her daily choice to pull her dark brown hair tightly into a bun on the back of her head. She has a standard uniform of a gun, badge, collared Polo shirt, and jeans. A sweater happens when it's colder.

Their dig location in the cemetery is as wide as a football field is long, and its length stretches even further. Approaching from the south, all the graves are to the left of the gravel road beyond the check-in tent. To the right, the day's workers are arriving, carrying what they will need for six or eight, or maybe 10 hours. They have cell phones and charging cords. Sunglasses and sunscreen. Raincoats and spare clothes. And, bug spray to deter a variety of biting Michigan insects.

Specialized teams begin to set up their stations with tables and chairs. Portable tents appear across the landscape. The tents will be lifted and moved around all day to cover open graves. They can help everyone escape the incoming rain, or the sunburn that comes from a week being outside. Team members pull generators and other equipment from the trucks.

What looks like kiddie pools for a backyard patio are set up so workers and all their clothing can be sprayed for decontamination before protective clothing is removed. Water pumps are pulled from storage bins and hoses are stacked. Someone has placed a bunch of color-coded sticks in a pile. Excavators rumble in. An emergency command post vehicle crushes the grass as it pulls off the gravel road, snapping a few tree limbs in its path. The brewing coffee begins to perk.

These exhumations are pursuant to a court order that Wayne County Assistant Prosecutor LaDonna Logan obtained. In her career she has never been asked to exhume so many bodies. Searches require 100 percent transparency for the courts. Shannon needs to be able to provide a list to LaDonna and the courts of who was there and what they took from the site. As more people arrive, Leslie yells out to everyone again to make sure they check in at the tent at the south end of the gravel road. There, two women sit with clipboards, recording everyone's name and affiliation.

In the first moments, they all appear to be a group of adults who could be waiting for a softball game or picnic to start. They chat and laughter is heard. They mill about on the gravel road before the briefing, some reacquainting themselves with familiar faces. Most come from the Detroit Police Department (DPD) and various FBI field office Evidence Recovery Teams (ERTs). Some are borrowed from other agencies for their skills. Many hold paper coffee cups—better to carry disposable items than to risk refillable cups getting contaminated.

Then they go silent. With her mission brief for the day's operation in hand, Leslie addresses the assembled agents and excavator workers alike. Her dyed blond hair is uncontrollably curly and falls like beach hair just above her collarbones. She is in her everyday uniform— badge, work pants, boots, an ERT t-shirt, and sunglasses. No gun today.

"Thanks everyone for coming," she yells to get everyone's attention.

As is the way of the FBI, she starts at the very beginning, briefing as if no one has any idea why they are there. "Detroit has hundreds of missing and unidentified persons cases," she explains. Their mission, she repeats to the group, is to "exhume bodies and obtain DNA samples to be compared against living relatives to reunite the families with their loved ones for closure and proper burial.".

In this third year of the dig, they hope to find more than two dozen sets of remains at Knollwood. All these murder victims were buried without DNA samples being taken because that wasn't an available option back then, she notes.

All have previously been provided the briefing paper she is waving in the air. It shows where to park, where to rally, where to find the port-a-potties, and where the Bone Tent is located. The Bone Tent is hardly more than a tarp over four poles with two tables underneath at the north end of the gravel road, but all eyes can't help but glance that way when it's mentioned. That's the goal. Everyone wants to bring bones to the Bone Tent.

If there are bones in evidence bags that make it to the Bone Tent, that means they have screamed loud enough for Shannon, Leslie, and the other women to hear their cries for justice. What exactly is justice for a person murdered? How can you mend the unmendable? They can't make full amends, but Leslie and Shannon know they can move the needle if everyone is willing to do their part on this messy, messy day. Many in this crowd have done this before and know what they must endure to get bones to the Bone Tent.

Leslie is Leslie thorough. "Potties are there," she points. "Hand-washing there. Taco boxes for today's lunch. Could be good, could be really bad," she says with a smile. "No weapons on the playing field so bench your weapon. No photography please. Do not do that. We have two photographers here. Grab a radio. We're on Alpha 1." The coffee truck is taking donations for charity, she reminds everyone.

She has an eternally optimistic tone about her, despite the subject.

"Our mission is to find 27 bodies in three days. If we do that, it will be an Operation United record," Leslie continues. "This is the best weather we've ever had, but it's Michigan. Watch ten minutes and it will change. It's going to rain, but it's not raining right now.

"So far we have six confirmed homicides victim names," she says spilling the beans on their DNA matches to keep everyone motivated. "Yes, Lori will have a radio," she says, "but we are not expecting her to answer. She is the Yoda of burial records."

This dig includes assignments for six search teams instead of the previous dig's seven, she notes. Four excavator operators from Detroit

Energy Company (DTE) join the group. "We could not do this without DTE," she says. "All the time and equipment." The hazardous materials team lead is from FBI Minneapolis, she notes, as she points out lessons learned the hard way. "Hydrate please. I'll ask you if you are hydrated enough and you'll say 'yes.' You're lying. Take breaks. Safety matters. We have three medics on scene. We'll watch for lightning"

She directs dig team members to walk over to don PPE. "We're not here to show how svelte you are," she jabs. "Pick something comfortable and use the buddy tape system."

To close the briefing, Leslie turns to Shannon, who is loath to speak to a person, let alone a crowd. She chokes out a quick but sincere thank you. Leslie closes it out by telling everyone to "find your team leader, be safe, be successful" and reach out to Leslie or Shannon with any problems or issues that arise. Leslie orders the team leaders to the Bone Tent.

The small group at the Bone Tent gets more details.

"As you can see behind you on the playing field there are pink tags on sticks." Everyone involuntarily turns to the field momentarily. "You'll get a full autopsy," she says, explaining that each person buried has a file with potentially, crucial information. She encourages them to use the information above ground to see if they have dug up the right person. "If someone is missing a leg, that's a clue. There is one baby today. We need the entire baby."

All are experienced at these digs, though for some, this is their first time leading a team. Protocols are repeated. Dig sites for each team are predesignated. All the teams are reminded they will be assigned to look for one body at a time, no matter how long it takes. Once a team thinks it might have access to the right skeleton, everything stops, and a call will go out to summon a forensic anthropologist to the site.

Team leaders are given metal clipboards attached to a metal container the same size, filled with paper and pens and their first file. Each dig involves a checklist to log the team members, verify photographs have been taken, and note the time a hole is cracked open and then closed. Leslie's team has prepared green cards with information to slide into body bags to explain what has occurred. Leave a card in the bag for the baby, she says, knowing there will be nothing left there if they are successful in finding the whole baby and take the entire remains.

Volunteers have brought coffee, breakfast food, and water. Excavators will do the heavy work of clearing grass and dirt and lifting concrete vault tops and caskets. Other volunteers have brought snacks and lunch. One team finishes installing a large, covered tent for lunch and protection from the expected rain. While some are still finishing a hand-held breakfast, a dozen or so move over to get their white Tyvek, sometimes Saranex, suits that are duct-taped to their bodies.

Leslie has scheduled her Hazardous Evidence Response Team (HERT) and other FBI "assets" to arrive there well before the main briefing. Among their tasks, is to be sure everyone gets synthetically made black or blue nitrile gloves, the tougher cousins of latex gloves usually worn in medical settings. It's a cool day and the potential rain will make the non-breathable suits uncomfortable to wear. But Leslie and Shannon would rather work in the rain. They don't like to, but it's better than the year before when a day turned unusually hot for Michigan and water became their most valuable player.

FBI Detroit has opened a 343G case, a police cooperation classification. It's the type of case any FBI office can open to document how they are assisting a local homicide investigation. The FBI tracks every hour that its personnel work, connecting it to a case or other official action. This will involve a lot of hours.

It's time to start digging.

CHAPTER 3

Broken But Still Good

Shannon applied to be a police officer with all the hopes of any recruit. She would care for the least fortunate and the city she grew to love. Shannon likes to take care of her people in Detroit even though most of them are dead and a few hundred were murdered.

Shannon knows she is broken in her own ways, but who isn't, she insists to herself. As with her adopted city, her work in the department allows her to find ways to rise above the fray. She desperately wants to change the ending to the story for those whose family members have been murdered. Right now it's just hard.

She was born in Royal Oak, Michigan, a town nearly as old as the nation itself and one of the many small towns that ring the city. It is home to her extended family, most importantly her mother and two brothers. Neatly mowed lawns and driveways filled with cars. The houses are Midwestern brick, some cinderblock, and lots of wood, brown painted wood. It had been its own town once, not part of the sprawling suburbs of Detroit. It is the result of families looking for cheaper homes and more grass to mow. Royal Oak also became one of many towns populated by Whites fleeing integration and fearing their Black neighbors. Their "safety" was secured with moves to Macomb or Oakland county communities just west and north of the city.

Shannon knows the life of a Detroiter from her work on the force. But she didn't come from there. Her Irish father and her mother, of Korean ancestry, wrangled Shannon's wild personality from the family's suburban home. There her chances for a quality education and a decent job were less impacted by the institutional racism and widespread segregation in neighboring Detroit, a blight of neglected streets, limited government services, few grocers, and little or no quality medical care for many.

A few miles south of her home, the landscape changes. No city limit signs needed. Here, empty lots and abandoned buildings remain a legacy of racial and class fears sprinkled with opportunistic government corruption. The streets have potholes that could swallow a car. Winter brings blissful relief from dirt-marred streets. Snow packs into the potholes and hides alleys filled with fast food wrappers, hugging 4-foot-high chain link fences used as property markers. Spring rains temporarily provide a cleaner canvas.

At Madison High School, Shannon was always busy doing something. She played softball and volleyball. Her taller, fuller stature enhancing the possibility of a win. She did try running track one year at Madison High School, but the student population was so small that in later years the idea of a track team finally had to be abandoned.

"If we had a home track meet, we would run over and do our event and then run back over to softball practice underway," she recalled. Mostly, though, she didn't have time for sports. She started working at 14. The money was helpful. She was good at going her own way. She doesn't need streets signs. They are part of her DNA. She grew up on these streets, a bit too scrappy. A bit too much to prove. But smart enough to keep quiet most of the time and prove her worth with actions.

The jobs kept her out of trouble and gave her pocket money. After graduation she tried selling jewelry, bartending, and even managing a restaurant. But the siren's song of the family business ultimately drew her in. Her father, a cop working in nearby Madison Heights; just one of many of the area's "finest." Her brother, uncle, and cousins too, had taken that path, serving in and around Detroit.

It was a way to fit in, or maybe just prove her loyalty to her clan.

The ninth police officer in her family, she sheepishly confessed she joined the academy hoping to keep her driver's license intact. She had "citation-producing driving habits," as she tactfully described them.

At the police academy she told no one that her father was a cop. She was his everything. Or the other way around. Each day the academy trained her to use a gun, fight for her life, and fill out paperwork. After class, she returned home to care for her frail and failing, larger-than life father who was awaiting a liver transplant. He stayed with her before the surgery. She'd pick up his medications and drive him to seemingly endless medical appointments.

It created awkward moments at times, but memories she could later hold.

The number one rule in a police academy is not to stick out. The arrangement was perfect for a comfortably solitary Shannon. But sometimes it wasn't fun. There were the times when she was razzed by classmates after her father called the office to let them know she was on her way but would be late.

"You got your daddy calling for you," Shannon would hear when she arrived.

There was no way to stop him from making the calls. In his mind, he was calling his old department friends. He still had all the old numbers memorized and would make the calls over her objections or without her knowledge. She had to learn how to administer intravenous medications daily to her father. It was time consuming and not always a smooth process. The classmates didn't need to know. She felt no compulsion to explain her late arrivals.

That care helped keep him strong enough for the surgery, and she was relieved when the time for surgery came. She was characteristically stoic. But transplants are complicated and not always successful. Within weeks, a sergeant showed up at the doorway of one of her academy classes. He needed to drive her to Henry Ford Hospital. It was time to let her father go.

Tradition and legacy go together in law enforcement. When a family member joins the force, it is often the proud uncle, brother, father, or mother, who step up at the graduation ceremony to pin on the new badge. But a month before Shannon's swearing in, her dad died and so did that dream. In 2000, she was pinned at the ceremony by her brother. Her Dad had been sick for a long time, but he lived long enough to know she would follow in the family business.

A self-acknowledged daddy's girl, his passing at only 58 years old was agonizing for Shannon.

So much left unsaid and undone. He never knew she would soon have two of her own girls to guide.

"It's like it happened yesterday," she said, pausing as her voice thinned. She repeated aloud, "It's like it happened yesterday, every … day."

The protective walls around her grew. She threw herself into the work. New officers work 9-1-1 calls for shootings and robberies. Wearing the DPD blue and carrying all that gear, she responded to her share of special operations. It takes toughness to survive on the streets of Detroit. She had that one down.

Then, a happenstance. She transferred to a job few asked for—the missing persons team of one. While others were being laid off as the city of Detroit filed for bankruptcy in 2013, Shannon clocked overtime to figure out her new post. It was not a super career advancing job, but it did give her a whole program to run as she liked, without discussions or decisions by others.

Her city was crumbling around her just like her marriage. She desperately wanted to find a way to bring calm to her hometown's chaos. She owed that to her dad. Truthfully, she needed it.

The reality of her job quickly came into focus. Detectives in precincts try to work most of the emergent missing persons cases. But when they run out of leads, and time, it is Shannon they reach out to. Her workload is filled with files you get when a beat officer has given up on a case. Take this "shit pile file" off my hands, she hears as she takes a file with no leads, an angry family in tow, and nowhere to go.

Missing often equates with murder; law enforcement just doesn't often say it aloud. So many people go missing each year that it's impossible to track them, not only in Detroit but elsewhere across the country. Lists of them appear on different web sites for police departments, on state and county lists, and on sites dedicated to separate causes, such as Indigenous people, those who are transgender, Blacks, victims of domestic violence, and foreign visitors.

When a person goes missing, law enforcement's job is to find an explanation. Take the case of Detroit resident Darcel Ward, who in 2021 was reported missing by her family just weeks before a court hearing against her abusive ex-boyfriend. Nearly a month later, Shannon and fellow detective Catherine Guillaumin had to tell the family Darcel wasn't missing, but that she'd been murdered—one of the most difficult things a police officer must do. But Shannon knows information is often all that the family of a missing person gets, and it's always better than the deafening silence of uncertainty.

From her desk in a converted hotel casino, Shannon began to piece together what it means to work the missing persons desk. While her fellow officers stopped by their desks to write reports, eat lunch and chat, Shannon's desk and its surroundings became more of a memorial of the often forgotten.

A mountain of items on the desktop hold either the most pressing matters, or just the most recent items stacked there. Phone messages to return mix with a proliferation of yellow pads. It's hard to tell for sure what might be old cases or new. Lining the too-narrow aisles between desks and the wall are tan two-drawer file cabinets. Overstuffed, brown squeezy folders—legal size—tower in a jumble on top of each cabinet, daring anyone to add another folder to the Jenga pile. Empty chairs and available surfaces are stacked with paper files, photos, and folders.

Desks for fellow officers crowd the open, carpeted area. A nearby wall has a five-by-eight-foot paper image of the city covered in plastic. Every day, red, yellow, and blue push pins are added to mark where overdoses have occurred.

Her files appear to be a mass of disorganization. There is no centralized matrix to keep track of, look for, or compare information on those who might be missing.

Who had done this job before and thought this was good enough? From her desk, her work overload is visible. Calling in others is not in Shannon's nature. She prefers going it alone. She's a thinker, not a talker. Her cacophony of thought is there, but all internal.

How many times has someone's family called the police to report that a child or partner has gone missing? She is surrounded by the files and can't really determine whether someone is looking for all these people. It would be impossible for anyone else to say. It was 2013 and it still seemed as if blind luck and coincidence are the best chances for finding someone.

She was learning that the police department's missing persons program was all smoke and mirrors.

More than 2,000 officers patrol the 139 square miles of Detroit. As she collects information about missing people, she accepts she needs more information before she can begin a search. If, for example, the 4th Precinct on 4th Street has a missing person, it was less likely that person would turn up 15 miles away in the 8th District on W. McNichols Road.

"I have to have spreadsheets and data and if somebody's missing," she realizes. "I need to know what area they are missing from."

She begins building her own worksheets in her fortress against the back wall. Information might be in other DPD files or brought to her by another investigator. It may be a case from outside the city. If something lead her to a medical examiner's (ME's) report, that report gives her height, hair color, and even gender and race if a body was found before decomposition set in.

The lists tell her, 'Okay, we have this many people missing in this precinct and here and here, and these have been found, and this is what we are still looking for.'"

She knows from her years on the force that many of the names may belong to murder victims not yet found.

CHAPTER 4

Motor City's Multiple Lives

Homicide is a familiar word in Detroit. Everyone seems to know someone who knows someone who's been murdered in a city known for murder.

Detroit's history is intertwined with homicide. In 1974, the city earned the moniker "Murder Capital of the World" after 714 homicides were recorded. It's a far cry from the 138 recorded in 1965. From then on, social and political turbulence contributed to the increase, with 686 murders in 1987, the year Shannon was born. And those are just the recorded homicides.

Detroit once claimed status as the 4th largest city in America, spurred to growth by European emigrants flocking there in the first couple of decades of the 20th century. The auto industry boomed when pioneers like Henry Ford, Random Olds, and Walter Chrysler revolutionized production. Good paying jobs followed. Henry Ford's assembly line cut the production of a single car from 12 hours to just over an hour and a half, but the work was tedious and boring. To keep workers from quitting, he cut their workday from nine to eight hours and nearly doubled their pay with a guarantee of $5 a day. The word spread and the city grew.

Domestic migration of Blacks and Native Americans from the South helped give more than 1.8 million people a Detroit address by the 1950s. But still, 84% of the city was White.

But after World War II, the White population in this newly nicknamed Motor City began to flee. Not just well-paid auto workers fled, but others too. Some were in search of more land. Veterans were lured by new homes that boasted a shower in every bathroom, a luxury they learned to enjoy while in service. City businesses and residential neighborhoods were abandoned. National advertisers and popular television shows idealized the perfect suburban family with a house, a lawn, a car or two in the driveway—and neighbors who looked like them. White servicemen bought homes in the suburbs, unimpeded by the redlining mortgage bans that blocked their fellow Black Detroiters. Veterans received military stipends and collected unemployment benefits provided by the 1944 Servicemen's Readjustment Act, commonly known as the G.I. Bill. Less affected by racially based university admission policies, these new suburbanites also were provided funds to attend college, buy books, and pay for tuition and supplies.

Those who remained in Detroit, particularly minorities, the working poor, and non-Veterans, didn't have those advantages. Poverty and crime increased. Jobs became scarce. The economy faltered, and tax revenues for police, city services, and education plummeted.

Long before Shannon joined the force, financially strapped homicide squads with overworked investigators concentrated by necessity on the low hanging fruit—cases where leads were more abundant and less resources were needed. Still true to modern investigations, when initial evidence is scarce, investigations go cold quickly. When a victim is unknown, few if any leads are available.

Homicides involving unidentified victims are the most difficult. The dried-out photos and faded reports end up in rarely-opened files. So many unknowns. How do you know who the person spent time with? How do you know what neighborhood to ask around in? Did they work at the gas station or the fast-food place on the corner? Did they go to school or live on the street?

It's hard to show around a photo of a dead and beaten person or shot up body parts memorialized on a ME's table.

In a notoriously segregated city with a nearly all White police department and a demographic that shifted decidedly Black, racism wasn't just a concept, it was a way of doing business. For decades, the prioritization of cases seemed to routinely start with the question: is the victim White and do they come from a "nice" home? Unidentified victims in a homicide investigation earned limited or no attention. The dead often remained unidentified and erased from history after they were zipped into a cloth bag at the downtown ME's office and loaded onto a truck with other unfortunates. Once a week or so, the truck would traverse weather-beaten roads to the countryside, its contents to be buried in county owned pauper plots on the edge of the county line, unmourned and alone. The number of graves grew to the hundreds.

In those decades after the Second World War, Detroit could have drifted from the national spotlight to become just another Michigan boom-to-bust town like Bay City or Flint. But its reputation as an influencer was running on two parallel tracks, both as a city in trouble and a city with a new moniker: Motown.

Music's destiny revived the city that had been drained of prosperity and hopefulness in just a generation.

Berry Gordy, Jr., who founded Motown, was the great-grandson of a White Georgia plantation owner and one of his Black slaves. The Gordys were proof that the risk paid off when Berry's father joined more than six million other Blacks who moved up from the south during what became known as the Great Migration. They came for good paying Motor City jobs and to flee oppressive Jim Crow laws and practices after faltering Reconstruction efforts.

The city's ever-increasing Black population was a leader in the creation of exceptional jazz, rhythm and blues, and eventually rock and roll. Fresh off serving in the Korean War, Gordy had returned to Detroit, first working at an auto factory, and then joining forces with family members to create the iconic Motown sound, a mix of soul and pop that they likely never envisioned would have its eventual impact. Borrowing $800 from a family cooperative on January 12, 1959, he promised to pay the money back at six percent interest within a year.

His closest collaborator, Smokey Robinson, became his lifetime business partner. After Robinson and his wife would audition potential singers in their living room, they would be sent to the Gordys. Gordy had worked on the assembly line, marveling how a pile of Henry Ford's metal went in a factory door and came out a car. He would do the same with his singers.

On Grand River Avenue, the Gordys lived on the second floor of a small house. On the first floor, they built out a waiting room in front, and a small studio in the back. The studio, barely big enough to fit a Steinway piano and set of drums, became the iconic Studio A. Endless Motown hits were recorded as singers stood on hole-filled linoleum floors below microphones strung from loose wires, just inches from one another. Before someone joined the label, the Gordys employed assembly line thinking, requiring each recruit to learn how to dance, sing, and dress. Potential stars had lessons in poise and manners. They were taught to move, keep their hands manicured, and wear proper makeup and hair. They were taught how to introduce themselves to everyone from presidents to royalty.

Willing to do what it takes, one by one the Gordys purchased the adjoining houses on Grand River to use as rehearsal spaces and to press and mail their own records. When Marvin Gaye couldn't make it home, he slept overnight on the mustard-colored vinyl couch in the office. The office had a cigarette vending machine and its own switchboard to allow those in the houses to reach each other quickly. They kept dimes on the top of the candy vending machine so Stevie Wonder could buy a Payday whenever he wanted.

The results were some of their first chart-topping hits like the Miracles' "Shop Around" and the Marvelettes' "Please Mr. Postman."

Through the 1960s, Motown and other labels under Gordy's control included a stunning lineup of talent that defined a generation and was never to be repeated. Among them, Michael Jackson and the Jackson 5, Diana Ross and the Supremes, the Four Tops, Stevie Wonder, Marvin Gaye, The Spinners, The Temptations, Martha and the Vandellas, and Gladys Knight & the Pips.

Motor City and Motown became synonymous, a relationship that was on full display to America in the iconic 1965 music video of Martha and the Vandellas performing their hit song "Nowhere to Run" perched atop the back seat of an under-construction Mustang convertible being tended to by bustling assembly line autoworkers at Ford's massive River Rouge plant.

Not far away, a teenage Aretha Franklin was singing in her father's New Bethel Baptist Church, where she would eventually record her first single. Her father, the Rev. C.L. Franklin, was pastor of the 4,000-member church on Hastings Street, a street that ran through the center of the Black Bottom district. The district's name was derived from the French who had settled originally on the dark marsh soil of the once-exposed River Savoyard. Around the time of World War I, the "War to End all Wars," European Jews thrived on Hastings Street. But in time it became known as the financial and cultural center for the city's Black population. The Rev. Martin Luther King, Jr. would preach at the church when he was in town. Stores and banks catered to their affluent Black customers.

King had initially given his famous "I Have a Dream Speech" after a march in Detroit in June of 1963, then recording it for posterity at Gordy's Studio A. Two months later, on August 28, he would deliver the same speech on the steps of the Lincoln Memorial in Washington D.C.

Collectively, there was a renewed feeling the town would rise to its prior glory days. But that was not meant to be. Changes made in the name of advancement and fiscal responsibility set the city on a collision course with its new and powerful musical voices. It began when President Dwight D. Eisenhower signed the Federal-Aid Highway Act of 1956, authorizing $25 billion in spending on an unprecedented federal highway project. The act directed the standardization and expansion of the federal highways that crisscrossed the country, ultimately changing ground transportation forever. It also authorized the purchase of land, sparking controversies in many cities where powerful landowners clashed with the politically unconnected. Highway construction began slicing through many of the poorest neighborhoods, where land was cheaper and dissenting voices could be ignored. As a result, dozens of Black urban communities were bulldozed in the name of progress.

Detroit was no exception. Hastings Street and other areas were slated for demolition. Even revered structures like New Bethel Baptist were expendable. The Chrysler Freeway construction crew razed New Bethel Baptist along with the entire Black Bottom and Paradise Valley neighborhoods. The loss of Black Bottom displaced the home of the city's growing jazz and blues community.

With freeways now a priority, long-relied-upon bus and trolley services were cut back. No bridges or walkways were built across the highways in those poor neighborhoods, seemingly tearing apart church communities and family neighborhoods forever. This town was all about cars. Businesses downtown and along the Detroit River and Lake St. Clair suffered. Crime and property vacancies created a ghost town of abandoned buildings ripe to become drug houses, targets for vandalism, and places to dump bodies. The city continued to falter.

Though she was not yet born, Shannon's future was forged by these changes to her city and the resulting growth of the homeless and unemployed. The desolation begets room to dump the unidentified dead and murdered. Police collect the bodies of babies, teens and adults from alleys, streets, and the adjoining river. Soon cold case homicides outpaced the ability to investigate.

When Shannon was just a toddler, in the late 1960s, much of the national news was dominated by summer race riots taking place in dozens of U.S. cities. Rioters demanded jobs, decent wages, racial justice, and better schools for minorities. Detroit's riots in the summer of 1967 were the most violent in the nation's history.

For four days and nights, news organizations memorialized a soot and flame lit sky overlooking the expansive glow of buildings ablaze, illuminating the inability of the police to control looting and property destruction. And violence was often dispensed by the police themselves with beatings and arrests. The furor was not quelled until Governor George Romney—father of future Sen. Mitt Romney—called up the Michigan National Guard to clear the streets with heavily armed soldiers and tanks. By the end, more than 7,200 people were arrested. The rioting killed 43 people, 33 of whom were Black. Those injured numbered more than 1,000.

An estimated 2,000 buildings were destroyed or damaged, leaving hundreds of people homeless, people who were already struggling to feed and house their families. Among the buildings destroyed, the new home of New Bethel Baptist Church, as well as other structures in the 12th Street area where the Black Bottom businesses had relocated after being supplanted by expressways nearly two decades earlier.

Criminal gangs began to take over. Property and business tax revenues plummeted. In the years that followed, nearly all the city's remaining White population fled to a promise of suburban bliss and a waste of vacant and decaying properties remained.

Dealing a crushing financial and symbolic blow to its birth city, Motown Records moved its operations to Los Angeles and left behind a row of empty promises on Grand River Avenue. With that, many said, Detroit lost part of its soul and seemingly left its best days behind, never to be reclaimed.

Once called the Jewel-of-the-Midwest, Detroit's population dropped below a million. Homicide rates tripled. Property values bottomed out. Hundreds of vacant buildings were available for drug houses, prostitution rings, runaway flophouses, and gang activities.

It became easy to drop a body in a building, alley, or even on a street. In and around this bleak environment, the number of unidentified homicide victims grew. Shannon's files originated from this place.

CHAPTER 5

Digging on the Farm

Leslie loves to dig things up, and, especially now, dead people. It began sometime before her tenth birthday when she decided she wanted to be an archeologist. Demanding and dogged, she planned for that career.

But more often now she can be found sitting in the FBI's Detroit office a few blocks away from the police station. She works alone at her desk, spending most days doing paperwork and arguing for funding so her forensic team can collect evidence for criminal cases in the state of Michigan.

The Michigan countryside is similar to her home state of Wisconsin. Like Shannon, Leslie stays laser focused. Growing up, socializing with friends or dating took a backseat to her curious nature and self-created solo expeditions.

On any given day when she was young, dirt from her parents' farm was ground into her tiny hands as she dug up long forgotten, buried treasures, some offered up from other temporary occupiers of the land or passing travelers. Others she provided.

"I was a farm kid, and I love digging, and so I would steal my brother's Matchbox cars, and then I would bury them in different parts throughout the farm. And then I would patiently wait all winter and come spring and summer, I would set up my little grid, and I would painstakingly excavate these cars out. Back then I was thinking, 'This is fascinating. I could totally do this for a living.'"

The farm she still loves so much isn't just the property where she grew up, it's her center. And the grid work proved to be prescient. An involuntary smile broadens across her face at the mention of the farm.

"Pure fun," she says as her eyes lose focus. She is back in the Midwest. "Pure enjoyment."

It is the quintessential Midwestern farmhouse, painted white on the outside with a front door, rarely opened. Instead, farmhouses beckon those who must enter to gain entry from the side door; into the parlor, as it were.

Walter and his wife, Patricia, and her much older brother moved to the farm before Leslie's arrival. The two-story house was forever being reinvented by her father. A sensitive and introspective man, Walter showered Leslie with love and attention in his quiet way. She was hard to say no to. He taught her to be respectful and honest, to farm, and to build anything.

Mostly they kept each other company on the isolated property near tiny Delevan, Wisconsin. The brother wasn't in it for the long haul. The farmhouse sits off a two-lane county road in the middle of well-manicured commercial corn and soybean fields. A stand of pine and deciduous trees along the east side of the dirt driveway and the west side of the property signals protection not just from the cold winds, but also from the dirt that inevitably wafts through the air during planting season.

A good walk could take you to another nearby farmhouse, but that's not likely to happen during the long and harsh winters when the arctic chill flows down from Canada. The winds whip across the flattened farmland and the snow they bring creates random snowbanks along the country roads that dissect the farmland.

When she was a child, a half dozen horses needed to be tended to at any given time. She learned to provide for them from the hay and oats grown on their land and baled on the crisp fall days. Five flat-as-a pancake acres provided Walter an opportunity to teach Leslie to saddle and ride. She will return to that farm one day.

The house is set back just enough to not be bothered by the cars speeding by, but not so far away that you miss a chance to wave at neighbors passing by—whether in a truck or combine.

Visitors pull up the gravel driveway and pop up the side steps, landing by the farmhouse table near an always-burning fireplace. A huge L-shaped kitchen counter that Walter built divides the room, and a back door faces out to the yard toward a small garage. It screams of an addition that came with the change to automobiles from horse and buggy days. Behind the house, the mandatory barn and a silo reaching skyward signals to drivers that they are approaching the farm. It's the kind of community where all the house doors remain unlocked, and keys are left with the farm equipment. The garage door is left open when you're not home, so if a neighbor needs to borrow a tractor or tool, they can just take it. It will come back, Leslie confidently explains.

Walter's construction business and Patricia's accounting practice paid the bills, but the farm was always the center. Together with Leslie, the couple kept the house in a constant state of remodeling, a condition that remains to this day.

Patricia was always a skilled baker and candy maker, and she shared her secrets and completed work generously as Leslie grew up. Christmas cookies required endless baking days and plenty of counter space to produce the enviable tray after tray. No one left the Larsen house without cookies shaped like hearts for Valentine's Day, or ghosts and pumpkins at Halloween.

The rebuilt kitchen was an early priority. Farm life permits the patience to bake traditional stews and roasts for supper that can only taste that good because of the time left in the oven.

Her interest in burying her brother's Matchbox cars under layers of loamy soil and digging up dead people grew from her time with both parents.

"I grew up in a very rural setting with not a lot of kids my age to play with, so I had to kind of rely on my own imagination and trips to the library to really create these worlds of fun," she said. Patricia loved reading and movies, and provided Leslie with a steady diet of adventures. With her folks working at home, Leslie was surrounded with the work ethic that ultimately earned her a spot in the FBI.

"My mom was an avid reader, and she loved adventure books and movies like *Indiana Jones*," she recalls "There was another one called *King Solomon's Mines;* it was kind of like the poor man's version of *Indiana Jones* adventure movies." Leslie found her own favorites. The *Goonies* movie is a tale of kids digging in caves for buried pirate treasure.

It was on one of her trips to the Whitewater Library with her mom that she hit the mother lode, her first book about Howard Carter, one of the most famous Egyptologists of the 20th century. A British archeologist, Carter earned worldwide fame when he led an expedition that resulted in the 1922 discovery of the intact burial chamber of the Boy King, Tutankhamun, in Egypt's Valley of the Kings.

Carter was her hero, and she spent as much time as she could score in the library falling in love with that period. They both aspired early on to be archeologists. He had spent his childhood wandering through Egyptian antiquities in a mansion near his home, and, by the time he was 17, he had secured a position on an Egyptian dig. In a career that was to span some 40 years, the discovery of the tomb was his pinnacle, and it took a full ten years to complete the excavation.

Her brother, Jeff, was eight years older and was less enthralled with her. Honestly, "He didn't really want anything to do with me," she recalls. She explored on her own, hoping against hope for an equally antediluvian treasure.

She searched for old arrowheads on the playground of Lakeview Elementary School. She explored a prehistoric Native American community that was preserved as a National Historic Landmark at nearby Aztalan State Park.

She found buried treasure in an old cistern on the property. "They were ancient..." she pauses, correcting herself, "I shouldn't say ancient 'cause they weren't ancient." The Depression Era glass prescription bottles were covered in years of grime, but she carefully took the needed hours to clean them and determine their origins. So precious a memory, her parents say they still can be found in the basement of the farmhouse. Soon she would dig everywhere. If her dad took her to a construction worksite, she would wander off to find a place to dig, even if it was an old dump site. Anywhere she could find dirt, she dug.

Remodeling expanded her room, making extra space for her growing collection of books about archeology, magazines on mysteries, and unearthed treasures. The small side porch made way for a winding wrap-around porch, luring visitors to sit a bit and forget about the outside world.

When Leslie wasn't entertaining herself on the farm, her mom would often drive her the ten miles to the mall in Janesville, where she would sit on a bench and watch people walking around. With each she would make up stories about why this person has a limp or that one was carrying a gun in their waistband. She eavesdropped on conversations and speculated on the task that wore out a person's clothes in a particular way. She imagined why someone chose a certain haircut or purchase.

As Walter's business grew, he converted part of the barn into his tool shed and office. At some point, no one had time for horses, so they were sold. It was by this barn that Leslie spent many hours during the summer before she started high school, banging a tennis ball against the side wall. She had run track in junior high, following the lead of her father who had lettered and held records at nearby Elkhorn High School.

She was fast and agile, but not a fan of most fall sports for women, so settled on the perfect solo sport of tennis. A $20 racket from the five-and-ten became her playmate, and she would batter a tennis ball from sunup until sundown against the side of the barn. Her mom signed her up for a city tennis lesson that took place all day. By fall, she was a freshman walk on for the Whitewater High School varsity tennis team, where older players welcomed her skills and mentored her.

Tennis became integral to her plan. Any cloudiness remaining in her crystal ball became much clearer in her freshman year when, on Valentine's Day in 1991, Strong Heart Productions released a movie based on the psychological horror thriller by Thomas Harris, *The Silence of the Lambs*. The movie pitted a young FBI agent trainee, played by Jodie Foster, against a serial killer and cannibal, Hannibal Lecter, played by Sir Anthony Hopkins. In a fantastical setting, Foster is assigned the task of hunting down another serial killer before he kills again. To succeed, she must engage in a mind game of matching wits with the jailed cannibal who is teaching her how to find a serial killer.

It was one of the rare occasions where the FBI allowed selective filming in FBI space, this one at the Bureau's training academy in Quantico, Virginia. In the opening scenes, Foster's character is seen walking through the Academy's large gun-cleaning room filled with black lacquer lab tables where agents stand to dismantle and clean their firearms. Later Foster is seen running on the training academy's iconic sign-filled trails. The movie went on to sweep the Academy Awards that year.

After seeing the movie at the Janesville theater, Leslie fell in love with it. When the movie came out on VHS tape, she convinced her parents to buy it for her so she could watch it repeatedly. It became her North Star.

CHAPTER 6

He Was Filleted Open

Suddenly, becoming an FBI agent went to the top of the list. She began her studies in criminal justice and psychology, using a tennis scholarship to attend Carthage College, a private college on the shores of Lake Michigan. Not long after she started college, serendipity placed her standing on the sidewalk in front of FBI Headquarters in Washington D.C.

The J. Edgar Hoover Building sits on Pennsylvania Avenue, halfway between the White House and the U.S. Capitol. The route is familiar to those who watched a new president travel from his swearing in at the Capitol to his new home at the White House. Halfway down, the motorcade travels past the Department of Justice headquarters on the south side of the street and FBI Headquarters on the north side. Tan concrete slabs surround an FBI building that was built in the late 1960s on an entire block of very valuable D.C. real estate. The building was designed to have public shopping spaces on the ground floor, with FBI offices on higher floors, looking down on a courtyard. Once the building was complete, Director J. Edgar Hoover refused to offer the retail space for rent.

Until the horrid United States terrorist attacks on September 11, 2001, the courtyard was open to visitors who could approach the reception office in the middle of the courtyard. It was located where knowing eyes could look up toward the 7th floor office of then-director Louis Freeh. Etched on a wall nearby, is former Director Hoover's philosophy and a statement every FBI agent knows to be true: "The most effective weapon against crime is cooperation. the efforts of all law enforcement agencies with the support and understanding of the American people."

One summer, Leslie found herself on that sidewalk with her mom after a day attending the National Youth Leadership Conference. She begged—can we just go see the FBI building? But when they arrived, it was her mother who pushed further, encouraging her to stop by the visitors desk to see about working there after college. Prepared for public inquiries, the receptionist pushed a piece of paper through the bulletproof glass–a brochure on how to become an FBI Honors Intern, that advertised a new summer program for students. Leslie was elated. She had nothing to lose. Her persuasive essay landed her one of the 97 spots offered to more than 23,000 applicants.

And there was more. On orientation day she was assigned one of the rare and coveted internship slots, but not at FBI Headquarters. Leslie would be sent to the new Profiling and Behavioral Assessment Unit at Quantico. The unit included some of the world's most respected behavioral experts at a time when they were beginning their research on serial killers and other criminals. Leslie already knew about many of those cases from her time spent in the library and from reading the news.

As a teenager, Leslie had convinced her parents to let her subscribe to a weekly magazine produced by *Life* that featured notorious serial killers and their gruesome and spectacular stories. The stories included the crimes of Jack the Ripper, Otis Toole, Jane Toppan, Richard Speck, and Ted Bundy. After all those years of reading about profilers working serial killer and murder cases, she was suddenly going to spend the summer working with the mythical creatures. These were the guys and gals really doing the work.

Leslie was in the room with profilers just a few days before the decision was made to arrest serial killer Andrew Phillip Cunanan, responsible for killing five, including fashion designer Gianni Versace and Chicago real estate developer Lee Miglin. Cunanan's victims came from different states, and FBI evidence teams helped sort out evidence while its behavioral experts worked on identifying Cunanan and determining why he was on a killing spree.

The internship blended her fascination with mystery and personalities and behaviors. Why, she wondered, do people think the way they do and do the things they do? By summer's end she was focused on finishing college and finding a job where she could both dig up dead people AND be an FBI agent. To her surprise, the Milwaukee FBI office recruiter, Irene Walker, called her immediately and offered a job at their office a few blocks from Lake Michigan.

Leslie's dream was coming true. She was being offered a job at the FBI, something only about three percent of applicants got. But she paused. To be a special agent, you need a bachelor's degree, along with three years of full-time work experience. The only exception was a 12-month break from the work experience requirement for those with a master's degree.

Leslie loved working the complicated serial killer cases. The idea of proving who murdered someone—or several people—was fascinating. She wanted that, but not yet. She needed to look down the road. She needed to finish university. She turned down the job. Solving murder mysteries, collecting evidence, and digging up the dead would have to wait.

With the FBI still in her sights, Leslie began a master's degree program at Marquette University while she was still finishing her undergraduate studies. Two jobs at a local shopping mall gave her little time to socialize, but they did pay the bills. These were jobs she gladly gave up when the FBI relented on her plan to finish school, and she was offered a job to sort mail into little metal slots in the upstairs mailroom in the FBI's downtown Milwaukee office.

Earning A GS-5 salary of less than $10,000 a year, she felt as if she had won the lottery. Her first steady paycheck was low stress as she took confidential trash to a trash burner, distributed mail, and occasionally spotted for the people who answered the main phone line to the public.

She joined the Evidence Response Team (ERT) and soon she saw her first dead body on a call-out to a Native American reservation. The man was filleted open, and blood was everywhere.

"That was the first time I had seen a body that looked like that, and I was fascinated. I was right in there, looking, smelling, taking it all in. I remember the dead truck arrived, and the dead truck back then was just the funeral home pick-up guys. They're like, 'We're not coming in there to get the body, 'cause it's covered in a pool of blood at the bottom of the basement stairs.'

"One of the guys on my team is outside throwing up and I'm like, 'Why is she getting sick?' The [team leader] is like, 'Does this.. None of this bothers you?'

'No,' I said.

'Perfect, he said. 'Put that body in the body bag and get it up the stairs.' One of my other teammates helped me pick up the body and we carried it upstairs and we put it in the dead truck. I'm thinking, this is fantastic."

Investigators followed the bloody footprints up a hill in the snow to solve the murder.

She learned the FBI inside out. Confidential trash—those papers too sensitive to put in containers–need to be picked up by local collectors to be pulped, shredded, burned, or some combination of the three. Answering the phone, even if filling in for someone, provided those first interactions with the public—the people the FBI serves and seeks to protect every day.

When she was bored, which was often, Leslie wandered among the aisles of dusty shelves of closed cases, studying the old case files of one type of investigation or another. FBI files are sorted by investigative classification. A bank robbery is a 91 case. If the person is armed, it's a 91A case. A violation of the Civil Rights Act of 1964 is a 173 case. A

164 is a crime aboard an aircraft. Each field office also has a two-letter file designation. So, a 91A-MW case is an armed bank robbery that occurred in the Milwaukee Division, which covers the entire state of Wisconsin.

In her spare time, she read files. She would start reading a 91A bank robbery file from beginning to end and then move to a new classification. She started reviewing files from different case agents to see who was doing it right and who had a lot to learn. She wanted to learn it all. She was anxious to become an agent, but only once she had learned everything there was to know about whatever job she was in. For Leslie, learning meant doing. She was not fond of management. "Managers may be nice people," she was heard to say on more than one occasion, "but managers are often a waste of resources."

Some employees remain in a particular job their entire career, but Leslie was a sponge. She volunteered for anything, and oftentimes everything, and switched jobs readily within Milwaukee's small complement of non-agent professional staff. She learned how to dispatch emergency calls and how to manage files. She took on the challenge of meticulously documenting electronic surveillance materials when a source is used to record a conversation about illegal activity. She moved over to the evidence room to learn how to properly bag and tag evidence to preserve it for trial. When her boss, Assistant Special Agent in Charge Jeff Berkin, suggested she train to become an emergency medical technician, an EMT, she spent the two years moonlighting after hours hoping it will enhance her agent application.

She began volunteering at a battered women's shelter. She didn't offer this information to her workmates, but instead would often just disappear after work, saying she was busy. It was particularly important to her, and personal. She volunteered as a counselor for the FBI's Employee Assistance Program (EAP). She wanted to be a profiler and was willing to do anything to get there.

But even to apply for a coveted special agent spot, you had to be 26. She was still too young. Investigating murders and digging up the dead would have to wait. There would always be dead people to dig up.

CHAPTER 7

The Harbinger

Leslie shifted her focus to work as an intelligence analyst, the last move before an agent application, she thought. She likely only had one shot to be accepted into a new agent's class. She needed to be competitive.

But she could not have foreseen how her side job on ERT would forever change her life. A gentle-guiding and always-smiling ERT leader, Special Agent Kent Miller, took her under his wing. He taught her the ropes early on as they searched the home of a man suspected of producing child pornography.

"I'd never been in someone's house before," she told a friend over lunch one day, reflecting on her first search and what led her to a job collecting evidence. "Kent said open everything with a door on it. I looked in the fridge and freezer. This guy has got all these animals that he let die, that were hanging out in his fridge, like turtles and fish, small animals. And I thought, what the heck?"

Five months after she completed ERT basic training, terrorist-hijacked planes hit the World Trade Center's Twin Towers in New York and the Pentagon in Washington, and crashed in a Pennsylvania farm field. She deployed to the Pentagon site, where she was assigned to handle EAP matters. But she quickly realized she was of little help in the trauma counseling area.

"I was a kid, what did I know?"

Instead, she slid over to assist the FBI's Washington Field office ERT team that was there to recover bodies and collect evidence. Four planes had gone down in three different areas of the country. The FBI was managing its largest and most far-reaching terrorist investigation ever. ERT teams from each of the FBI's 56 field offices were deployed to collect evidence and help the recovery effort. She soon departed Washington D.C. -- but not to return home. She was diverted with the Milwaukee ERT to the much more challenging New York recovery scene.

Two planes had crashed into the iconic Twin Towers, killing thousands, and toppling multiple buildings. Local and national officials were overwhelmed by the debris field and the remains of thousands of bodies on the lower west side of Manhattan in an area quickly designated: Ground Zero.

With no place to sort the Manhattan site carnage, the city shipped the debris from Ground Zero via barge 30 miles downriver to Fresh Kills, a closed landfill on the shore of Staten Island. The puzzling name for the site has its origins in early settlers. Fresh Kills is a Dutch derivation of a word meaning waterway. The landfill had been capped because of the dangerous methane that had collected underneath. Leslie recalled appreciating the methane threat after she saw a union guy jump from his excavator cab and break into a full run when he thought he hit a methane pipe. Taking no chances, the Milwaukee team fled too.

FBI teams from across the country joined other evidence experts, rotating in a few weeks at a time, to allow for 24/7 processing of the remains. Work was by hand and uncomfortably intimate. The unyielding smell of jet fuel permeated their personalized protective equipment as they picked rings, photographs, and human remains from the debris.

"At that point it was pretty new," she said of the process. They were doing what they could with the tools they had. The FBI's largest field office, not far from the Twin Towers, was damaged in the attack and unavailable. Field office operations had shifted to a large FBI garage facility on 26th St. in Chelsea that had wide open spaces where mechanics maintained the office's fleet of cars.

"We were laying out debris fields and the early part of our tenure up there kinda raking through things. Then they switched us to these recycling sifters, so they would scoop things up, dump it on the recycling sifter."

As the conveyor belt sent debris past, they did their work.

"We'd have buckets down below and we'd have a bucket for body parts, a bucket for sensitive information, and a bucket for money, and a bucket for any personal items that we could get identified and possibly clean and returned back to the family," she said. "Every so often, people would come by and empty out the buckets and then give us fresh buckets."

Several government agencies, including the Secret Service and the U.S. Mint, had offices in the buildings that collapsed, and they were on the lookout for sensitive materials.

They dropped body parts and plenty of random bones into containers along with scalps and intact rib cages.

"Yeah, I don't eat ribs to this day, that's my–I have two hang-ups from 9/11–I don't eat ribs, I don't wanna be around anybody that's eating them. We pulled out just a boatload of intact rib cages, and somehow my brain is associating an intact human rib cage with ribs that you eat, so I just choose not to eat that."

Another trigger, the smell of jet fuel at night. She worked with protective equipment most of the time at the Pentagon and Fresh Kills, but not all the time. Now, she is one of the more than 70,000 people in the World Trade Center Health Registry, tracking the chronic and fatal illnesses and mental health recovery progress of first responders, victims, and survivors. Federal and local assistance includes free mental health counseling and medical screenings.

Most people working at the FBI and other responding agencies during that time have former co-workers who've died. Leslie is no exception, aware that more than two dozen FBI agents and professional staff who worked at the crash sites have already died, she knows doubtless more will follow from resulting cancers.

The work at Fresh Kills hardened and matured Leslie. Her idyllic life in the upper Midwest now was only part of her being. The carnage of war scarred her, but it emboldened her, too, to not let anything or anyone step between her and the victims she swore to protect. Everyone talks about taking care of victims, but at Fresh Kills every item Leslie touched was not an item, but part of a victim. It wasn't enough to avenge their deaths, these silenced victims deserved the tenacity of every living person who could speak for them. It was a weight she simply had to carry after that.

Living life became so, so important. She became more decisive, surer of herself, and returned to Milwaukee an eager, but no longer naïve, mail clerk. Within a few years, she was in Quantico, Virginia, training to be a special agent. As if that wasn't surreal enough, she soon found herself walking through the same gun cleaning room and running the same trails actor Jodie Foster traversed while filming Silence of the Lambs.

By 2005, Leslie was a newly minted agent in the Detroit field office. Though she could have been assigned anywhere in the country, she was pleased with that ticket. The farm was a sixish-hour drive, depending on traffic in Chicago and that always-traffic-filled highway drive around the south end of Lake Michigan. Winter provided a bit of an extra challenge with the blowing wind and additional lake effect snow that often covered the highway. Her parents helped her pick out a house to buy and remodeling the new home brought the Larsen construction team back together again.

ERT work quickly overtook her desire to work investigations. ERT work is considered an ancillary duty, which means you work cases, also criminal and terrorism alike. In her first year, she was part of the team literally taking down a barn north of Detroit in one of the many futile searches for the body of former Teamsters chief and convicted felon Jimmy Hoffa. Though the office has searched many sites, the body of the celebrated kidnap victim has never been found. When search warrants were being executed or a team callout was necessary because of an agent-involved shooting, Leslie was out the door.

Leslie's organizational skills and self-discipline made her shine. She played tennis incessantly to make it on the team. She volunteered for everything to make her agent application as strong as possible. When she didn't have enough to do at the Pentagon disaster site, she joined in on evidence collection. In Detroit, she quickly became frustrated at the undisciplined and sloppy methods she felt were utilized by their ERT. She offered to lead training, relying on her own training to try to make the team more productive and professional.

Leslie first took, and then taught, all kinds of training. ERT members need to know how to take photographs, to draw and to grid crime scenes, and complete paperwork. They collect bullet casings and fragments, drugs and drug paraphernalia, finger and palm prints, and blood and other body fluids. Evidence admitted at trial needs to stand up to courtroom challenges, demanding that it be gathered methodically and consistently, whether collected in the rain, under water, in the snow, or from underground.

Understanding how to dig up a body or anything underground is its own skill, so Leslie learned from the experts at the Body Farm in Tennessee, aptly nicknamed for its devotion to the study of human fossilization, or human taphonomy. The Body Farm is really named The Forensic Anthropology Center at the University of Tennessee. It's led by five women recognized as among the best in the world at analyzing evidence of human remains that are discovered partially or fully underground. The Center takes donated bodies and uses them to train medical and law enforcement professionals in the disciplines of body decomposition, remains recovery, and other areas, such as distinguishing human bones from those of animals.

It was her first encounter with strong organizational leadership that was almost entirely made up of women. About 15% of the FBI

Special Agent workforce was female at the time, and that number was well below 5% when counting only upper management.

Leslie devoured the Body Farm courses and demanded more. She found another twist on dead body recovery in her home territory when she met Dr. Jane Wankmiller Harris at Northern Michigan University. Jane works with frozen bodies. Another female leading the way. Working in the Upper Peninsula, Jane is the director at FROST, an appropriate acronym for the Forensic Research Outdoor Station. It is the only other location in a northern climate dedicated to studying human taphonomy.

Michigan is the largest state east of the Mississippi and about half of its 100,000 square miles is covered in forest. Geographically, the state is two peninsulas, referred to locally as the Upper and Lower Peninsulas. The UP was acquired as part of a land squabble with Ohio shortly before Michigan became a state in 1837. In the deal, Ohio acquired a small southern strip of land that included Toledo, and Michigan added the entire Upper Peninsula. Michiganders knew they got the better end of the deal.

Michigan's FBI office has always had its share of bodies to dig up, and team callouts are part of the team's activities. The Detroit team is often on the road since it has investigative responsibilities for the entire state of Michigan, a 650-mile trip from the southeastern-most point of the Lower Peninsula to the western tip of the Upper Peninsula.

Leslie learned as she went. On Christmas Day 2009, she and others were called to Detroit Metropolitan Airport to preserve evidence from the inside of a Northwest Airlines Airbus 330 after a Nigerian passenger unsuccessfully tried to set off chemical explosives someone had sewn into his underwear as the plane attempted to land.

The "Underwear Bomber," as the case became known, is believed to have acted at the direction of a Middle Eastern terrorist group, something the bomber admitted when he later pled guilty and was sentenced to prison for life. Collecting evidence aboard a large jetliner in an airport, and from passengers anxious to get home on Christmas Day, was messy. The case was one of many challenges the team faced that year. It was a tough year, and they did some stupid things, she recalls. But they learned a lot.

By March of 2010, the woman who eschewed management was promoted to lead Detroit's 24-member team, one of only five full-time ERT leaders across the entire FBI workforce now numbering nearly 40,000.

"I called the team together and I had a town hall meeting, a very honest, raw meeting with the team, and said, 'Let's talk about what we want this team to look like in the future. How do you wanna be thought of? What do you want your reputation to be as a team? What do you want your operational tempo to be? What kinds of callouts do you wanna go on? Let's build the team how we want the team, and we'll go from there.'"

Dedication and skills improved. They had to. When a train or plane crashes, it is FBI evidence teams that collect the evidence at the scene to support the National Transportation and Safety Board investigations. They are the only investigative teams working on all hazards, including shootings, bombing, nuclear threats, and other hazardous materials.

Soon Leslie had gathered a 40-member team, the third busiest in the FBI, that collects evidence at crime scenes around the world to be used in cases involving terrorists, drugs, bank robberies, and major white-collar prosecutions. Many team members have studied or even taught at the Body Farms, learning the intricate skill of pulling bones, skin, hair, fibers and more out of dirt, mud, and even snow and ice. Eventually the calls come not only for training, but for consults or assistance on challenging cases from seemingly everywhere.

Hazardous materials specialists work alongside experts in print lifting, photography, and crime scene reconstruction. Now they are among the world's leading forensic experts, teaching at the FBI Academy, the FBI Lab, overseas, and at body farms in Tennessee and Michigan. Leslie's team remains in demand.

Those nearby may say it's disgusting work. Those who do it say they love it. They dig bodies out of walls and concrete, and once, in a particularly gruesome case, improvised to manage a nightmare when a search resulted in the discovery of hundreds of human heads, breasts, and other body parts in one building.

Leslie has a deep bench and can call on many experts in forensic anthropology when any need occurs. Talents such as the women at the Body Farm, and Jane from the FROST Center, bring years of experience to a murder investigation. As experts in human skeletons, anthropologists train to provide weighted opinions on whether a skeleton or even a bone may be from a person with certain attributes. They may be able to estimate the age of the person, as well as height, facial features, and many other things that may lead to an identity. This is important when the bones of an unidentified person are unearthed.

When a doctor also can see damage to the bone, they may be able to say with near certainty that a victim was murdered.

CHAPTER 8

The Pauper Dilemma

Most civilizations have taken the responsibility to bury the unidentified, the poor, the unclaimed. These places are known by many names; a cemetery, a potter's field, a pauper's plot, a churchyard, and a graveyard among them.

The term potter's field originates from several references in the Christian Bible. A potter's field was said to be the place where Judas Iscariot was buried after he betrayed Jesus. The name has a literal meaning, taken from several references, including in the Gospel of Saint Matthew. In ancient times, potters would dig for high-quality clay to produce their wares. The holes they left in a field were available for purchase. Ancient writings says that potter's lands were purchased to bury the indigent and unclaimed. The Christian Bible tells the story of this type of land being purchased using the silver Judas accepted as payment for betraying Jesus.

Whether on ecclesiastical or government land, the dead were often looked after with a long-held belief that every person deserves a burial. Burial sounds ceremonial, though, so perhaps buried will do. It's a word representing the practicality, as opposed to a magnanimous gesture. After someone dies, though, no matter the cause, religious beliefs, or wealth, bodies need to be buried. Death spreads disease, and disease begets more deaths. The quicker someone is buried, the better.

In fourteenth-century Europe, more than 25 million people died from the global bubonic plague, or Black Death. Some estimates say 30 percent to 60 percent of the European population and a third of the population of the Middle East perished. Mass graves and graves loaded with multiple caskets were a necessity as the world managed multiple pandemics and outbreaks of the flu and tuberculosis. Most were known, some were unknown. In those days, communicable diseases spread like a strong summer breeze, whether through infected animals, flying insects, or contact with the dying. Efforts to contain these diseases sometimes included prohibiting infected bodies from being buried in private cemeteries and instead, bodies were heaped into deep, crudely dug pits. Church land was always a practical solution, if not elegant. But it was only for believers.

One record from 19th century England explains how church workers dug graves for paupers, some 50 to 60 feet deep, stacking wooden box upon wooden box until a dozen or more filled the grave. The stench of decomposition was so overwhelming that one coroner's inquest indicated a grave digger for Aldgate Church in London died from the poison gas being emitted, probably when he went down into the hole. Adding lime to hasten decomposition was common, but not always a solution. Shallower graves had been dug in past years, the inquest notes indicated, but deeper graves were needed when land around churches became a premium.

Though the wealthiest landowners had the means to bury their dead privately, many, many more bodies were routinely buried in public cemeteries. Graveyards for indigent paupers lay at the outskirts of most communities, a practice adopted in the new world, America. Practicality played a role. After the 1871 Chicago Fire that killed about 300, more than 100 were buried as "unknowns" in the county cemetery.

New York City, one of the country's oldest settlements, has about 20,000 paupers buried beneath what is now Washington Square Park, near New York University, on the southern end of Manhattan. The land was acquired for 5,000 graves, but when the city's residents suffered through a terrible yellow fever outbreak, necessity demanded body stacking, according to New York Public Library researcher Carmen Nigro. The city eventually began to and still buries anyone in its charge on Hart Island, home to an estimated one million graves, according to public city records. People suffering from yellow fever and tuberculosis victims were isolated on Hart Island, many who eventually died and were buried there.

The fear of spreading diseases often prompted orders that certain bodies be buried in these mass graves or graveyards. Before medical advances, those who contracted HIV/AIDS died a slow and painful death, surrounded by people who feared they could suffer the same fate if they had contact with the syndrome that became a worldwide epidemic in 1981. Hart Island became the destination for many with the disease and likely houses the largest concentration of AIDS-related burials. The city has a little discussed and ghoulish practice of "recycling" graves after 25 years. The practice of burying a new corpse over a decomposing body resulted in new spaces available when the 2020 COVID-19 pandemic struck. Thousands of the city's nearly 80,000 recorded COVID-19 deaths were buried on Hart Island.

As organizations in New York work to identify and better track historical burials, one organizer spoke of the humanity to the Washington Post in 2020, saying unclaimed "doesn't mean the person was unwanted."

The challenge is universal. The first two years of COVID-19 killed several thousand in Detroit and Oakland County, too, but this was not the area's first effort at managing mass graves. In the 1830s, Detroit had 5,000 residents and officials recognized swiftly that its 30-foot-wide cemetery, the city's first, was filling too quickly. In 1834, a second plot was purchased in the midst of a second cholera outbreak that spanned three years. The 33-acre Russell Street Cemetery opened. One estimate tallied the cholera deaths at more than 12 percent of the city's population. No one knows for sure, however, as historical files indicate the cemetery records were lost or most likely never properly completed. This created the now-too-familiar problem of bodies stacked on top of one another, with few ways to identify or distinguish one decomposing body in a box or cloth bag from another. Few, if any, grave markers were placed and little evidence exists to record even the most basic information, such as how many bodies were below, let alone the names of the deceased.

The Russell Street Cemetery was located where today's Eastern Market is in Detroit, just two miles north of Shannon's office in DPD headquarters. When that cemetery filled, the mayor ordered it closed, and a 300-acre cemetery, eight miles downriver, was opened that still operates today.

Many cemeteries are a mix of identified and unidentified people. In New York, many identified people are buried on Hart Island, too. Sometimes a known person has no known relatives, and the city handles the cost of the burial. Other times, the family cannot afford a burial, or the person who died or was found murdered is unknown. The task of handling the body is left to the city. The same is true in Detroit and in hundreds of other cities across the United States.

Many large U.S. cities, including Detroit, Chicago, and Los Angeles, initially built cemeteries on vacant land by the city center, only to find the city's growth demanded another plan. When hundreds of graves were ordered relocated from Detroit's two city cemeteries, historians acknowledged the likelihood that all were not accounted for in the move. "Are some still buried where Eastern Market stands?" one Detroit historian asked rhetorically in a local news story about the Russell Street Cemetery. Answering her own question, she added, "The probability is high that there are indeed still human remains there. Such is the case with any large city. All big cities are dotted with random buried corpses from centuries past, hidden under modern-day structures like skyscrapers and apartment buildings."

As Detroit's population grew, the number of paupers' graves outgrew the first section of the modern county cemetery. Pauper burial operations were moved to the vast expanse of United Memorial. The nearly century-old cemetery boasts 108 tree-lined acres. Rich or poor, young or old, many buried have oft-forgotten stories.

Among those buried using public funds, hundreds of Detroit's unidentified homicide victims who have involuntarily joined identified paupers and the indigent in the truck that travels to this cemetery. Most were unceremoniously dropped into a dirt hole. It's hard to know for sure unless you go back into the ground and try to find them.

News reports over the years show multiple lawsuits have been filed against the city, county, and Detroit cemetery owners after family members were unable to find gravestones they had purchased, were not allowed to watch the burial of their family member, or found missing or moved gravestones when they returned to visit. Many burial companies filed for bankruptcy. Detroit is not unique in that embarrassment.

Once buried, there may be few records available to confidently assure the public who is buried where. Often dirt roads worn down by use and aisle markers are only starting points. In many cemeteries, raised gravestones have deteriorated, been broken, or been moved. Some are removed to make way for flat markers that can be mowed over to reduce maintenance costs. When visitors to the cemetery pull off the gravel roads to move off the throughway, they sometimes drive right over markers and graves. Through the years, regulations have varied, with some requiring burials in a fortified vault, while some might be buried in a pine box or simple cloth bag.

Graveyard management is a tricky business. Cemetery plots are for a single person to be buried in a single spot under ground, leaving fewer graves to manage. Though all cemeteries have those burials, many also have managed burials for the paupers, those who are indigent and those unidentified, including murder victims. Those unfortunates are often stacked on top of each other. Either way, for a century, paper records have been the standard tracking system. But paper fades, gets damaged, and gets lost. Modernization through digital records has helped some, but those in the ground now gain no such benefits. Unless someone marks a grave, for example, with a GPS coordinate, it is hit-or-miss to go back and hope to find the same person you put in the ground. And, what might be found below ground has been impacted by the dedication or disregard of those running the cemeteries, exacerbated by the challenges of pandemics and plagues, shifting land, and changing government budgets.

A lesson both Shannon and Leslie would learn soon enough.

CHAPTER 9

A Box Castle

The boxes surrounding Shannon's desk create a feeling of solitary confinement. Although the detective bureau has some tall fabric room dividers that feign privacy between groups of desks, her collection of files makes them unnecessary. The banker's boxes line the floor where her feet belong. Rows of boxes four high are behind her along a wall.

They didn't start out all over her personal space, but she found that once she pulled a missing person or murder file from the warehouse it became hard for her to put it back. The office tells the story of a caretaker who believes each person deserves dignity, the right to be found, whether in the ground or still walking above.

Riled by the disorganization, she began working on a spreadsheet for missing persons. First, she added any name where someone had opened a file or received a call about a person who went missing. Shannon could find many of the details from the files. She recorded what she could about the missing person; name, address, last known location, friends, interviews conducted, photos, clothes they were wearing, jewelry, bags they were carrying, vehicle details, and school and work connections.

Dental records or a blood type might help solve a murder, but they are often not requested. Police investigators were likely called to the scene for a missing person case, not a murder. No need to unnecessarily frighten the family about the possibility that their missing loved one might be dead.

She realizes the oldest files are the sad stories of the long missing. They speak to the time, effort, and money police put in on any given case. Some are faded and have hand-scrawled notes on slips of paper attached. Who was really looking for that homeless Black man who died of a head wound and exposure in that back alley off Warren Avenue in 1968? Nobody. Who was hunting for a teenager gone missing in 1982? Surely, she was just a runaway who belonged to no one. Maybe she was a drug addict?

Shannon has learned some people don't want to be found. Maybe they were fleeing an abusive spouse or money troubles. Maybe they have legal problems. No matter, she adds the names to her growing list of the missing because someone asked DPD to look for them.

Each time useful investigative leads are exhausted, old cases are relegated to the cold case world. Shannon quickly learns that for decades after most of the world had entered the computer age, investigators in cash-strapped Detroit remain paper bound. Investigators have no way to search electronically to see if some investigative clue found today might match a cold case from long ago. When Shannon's daily work involves an older case, she treks nearly 20 miles to an overwhelmed storage facility to paw through endless, dusty investigative files. The converted grocery warehouse is lined with too tall wire racks jammed full of all the Wayne County files, and not just those from DPD. Packed like sardines, they are reminiscent of the images from the closing scene in the first Indiana Jones movie. Each lead has its own challenges, and every missing person case seems to need to be started anew.

Sometimes other law enforcement agencies call asking if their dead body is her missing person. Maybe there was a clue found in a pocket. She starts with the date the body was found, and begins pulling her cold case homicides and missing person files, one after another, looking for any potential match around that date. It works sometimes, but not often.

There is no process. When someone does come to her office about a long-ago missing person, they want to know what's being done to find that missing person. But she knows that the truth is that all those cases are inactive and nothing is being done. And the more Shannon travels to the old grocery warehouse, the more obvious it becomes there are two types of missing person files. Within those old crumbling files, she comes to recognize that overwhelmed investigators might have ignored missing person files that might match what she eventually calculates are a few hundred cold case homicides.

Unidentified homicide victim files begin to add to the morass around her. Most provide scant details compared to the other files. This person was beaten to death. That person was shot to death. Someone was injured and apparently left to freeze during the brittle Michigan winter. Others were thrown into the river, only to be fished out by police days or weeks later.

If a body is located, certain protocols had to be followed, including an independent evaluation by the ME. Nearly all the files include a ME's report that can provide some of the best leads. Examiners determine cause of death. The file coversheet blares out "homicide" and shows who died from a gunshot or stab wound, blunt force trauma, or other types of violence. Closeup photos of bullet wounds through the skull are clipped to full length various and detailed autopsy photos along with close up views of a naked body on a metal examining table. More tidbits for her list.

The ME might take dental impressions and fingerprints, but those will prove little value to investigators unless a potential match is available. Still the file might reveal some other useful investigative clues: personal possessions found on a body. Shannon chronicles each detail to make her list more comprehensive. Where were bones and other body parts found? What type of foul play was suspected? The unsolved murders often date back to the 1960s or earlier and include adults and kids.

When she started missing persons, she did not put a lot of emphasis on the unidentified bodies. Occasionally a homicide detective would come asking if she had a missing person that matched a body that had been found. She asked around, learning the cold case homicides were in files in the warehouse. She feared no one was working those homicides.

She'd look over her list or maybe head to the warehouse. Initially she presumed the missing person was likely still alive. But time taught her to add to her routine check the likelihood that homicide victims with no names might also be a match. With nothing electronic she had to pull a file jacket and paw through paper she knew no one likely touched since the jacket was boxed for the warehouse. Working a missing person case or a homicide case is nearly impossible without basic information, starting with a name, followed by a person's height, weight and sex. Identifying clothes, pictures, or dental records are bonus items.

A new twist seems to be around every corner. Even if a file she finds in the warehouse evidences a murdered woman, she comes to appreciate that there is only a slim chance that they have a matching missing person report filed from when the woman disappeared. Maybe the woman was alone, and no one even noticed she was missing. Maybe the murder victims or unidentified persons aren't from the Detroit area. Shannon quickly realized she also needs to collect information on unidentified homicide victims.

Her spreadsheets begin to expand as she adds the cold case homicides. She decides she needs two lists: one with the names and information about missing people and another with the unidentified dead bodies and body parts. She tracks down notes written on scraps of paper on her desk and in the drawers and adds them to the lists.

She finds details on the missing from a notebook she has here, and other information written on a file jacket there. Files might have a photo of the missing—a birthday party milestone, high school graduation, but more often a blurry Polaroid photo taken at a backyard party or at a picnic on Belle Isle. All the faces are smiling because they do not know their fate. Often the details are thin. But sometimes files include a description of clothes someone might have been wearing when they disappeared, or jewelry, or something found in a pocket.

Many are babies from the 60s and 70s who died because of neglect or lack of medical care; that's murder to a ME. Those baby cases inherently have less evidence connected to them and fewer lead opportunities. Babies have no shoe size, reading glasses, particular hair style, or distinctive clothing. Even finding a photograph in a file is unusual. And naked newborns have little, if any, hair. Unknown Baby Girl #1 was found frozen in an alley. Only the location might expose the adult who left the baby there to die.

Many child homicides were from the time before Roe v. Wade, the U.S. Supreme Court case that for 50 years gave women more autonomy over their bodies and their pregnancies. Unwanted or unexpected pregnancy might be the result of sexual assault, rape, or incest. Some overburdened families can't handle more kids. Fearful of no medical or legal options, girls were left to gave birth in bus station bathrooms and left their baby to die in the toilet of a public restroom or had a child in a basement and then "disposed" of it.

Identified only as a number, the baby homicide files are intertwined with other cold case homicides. They chronicle abandoned babies battered by abusive caregivers, malnutrition, drug overdoses, or exposure during long cold winter nights in the northern city.

As Shannon becomes absorbed in her job, she finds the number of unsolved murders had increased annually, including many who were buried without a name. Now, hundreds of paper files exist, not just of her missing persons' cases, but also of many unidentified people, many of whom are homicide victims. She thinks, where are these people and are there still families looking for them? She is consumed by the thought of children who have a missing parent who has never been found. How devastating it must be for a person to come home from work and find the dirty dishes and unfolded laundry, but the loved one missing.

As a child, she could be lost among the more boisterous boys and many extended family members. How fast would someone realize she was missing, she has thought occasionally.

Her imaginary business card morphs from missing person detective to matching living and dead persons to their names. She begins spending her free time looking through the homicide files for the unidentified. They aren't exactly missing person cases, but they are homicides that needed to be solved, and the victim had not been identified. Some of those people might in fact match her missing person files. She begins to learn that these are the toughest cases.

When police start with bones, even race and gender can be a challenge. Sometimes the entire body is found. Other times it might be just part of a body. A foot. A hand.

"The anthropologist may tell you female, male," Shannon says. "They'll try to give you some ancestry on it so you still try to break it down, but unless somebody is really young or somebody is really old, you got that middle age bracket where they can say this body is somewhere from 25 to 99 years old.

"It may be a skull that was recovered and that's it," She explains to those willing to listen. "It's more common that you'd think. So, I don't know how long that skull has been there. It could have been there 10, 20, 30 years. I can't single out which body is it going to belong to, which missing person is it gonna belong to.

It's hard, she adds in a whisper, as if realizing it for the first time. It's a rare display of emotion and reflection. She never appears to be judging, but occasionally can be caught simmering. Her shield is her solo pursuit of work.

Each year, more cases remain unsolved than the year before, and soon she has hundreds of outstanding cold homicide and missing persons cases. Now, she is surrounded by victims and the road to help them is blurry. Sometimes records are stuffed with all kinds of clues, like photos and personal possessions. Some files have indicators that

DNA had been taken and placed in the available federal file to search. Those are the best, with the big letters DNA stamped two-inches high on the front of the file jacket. Unfortunately, most of those cold case homicide files for the unidentified dated back to a time before DNA testing was available. And, once DNA testing entered common use in the 1980s and 90s, decision making no doubt included a calculation on which cases deserved the scarce resources. She realizes the truth, that DNA searches were often reserved to confirm an identity when police had other leads that justified the several thousand dollar cost.

As the tally on missing and unidentified babies and adults increased, so did her spreadsheet details. No matter what list they ended up on, Shannon's new spreadsheet had a few files with the DNA stamp and more still needing it. DNA was still new to Detroit police investigations. Few, if anyone, who was reporting a missing relative would also have a DNA profile handy. Even fewer would have their own DNA for matching unless someone in the family had had an interaction with the law, or more unlikely, had decided to spit into a cup and mail it away for an expensive DNA test.

Obtaining a DNA sample was not on the to-do list for processing unidentified bodies in the ME's office. Not long into her tenure, she recognizes that was one thing she could fix. Maybe she could stem the tide of non-DNA cases. She drafts a policy that requires DNA collection before any unknown person is buried or cremated and pushes it through management.

At least now, way before a body is turned over to the county for burial, a DNA sample will be taken. Though not fail-safe, it may be a good way to connect people in her spreadsheet as it continues to grow.

CHAPTER 10

The Confusing Blessing of DNA

Once a body is buried, the body begins to decompose, and with that, investigative clues begin to disappear.

Police reports on homicides for the unidentified provide limited clues to a person's identity. An autopsy report may describe the person as Black or White, young, or old, blond, or brunette. A few might include dental images taken in hopes of making a match to dental records. Bonus assists for investigators if documentation notes unique items such as a photo, glasses, clothing, shoes, jewelry, and other personal items. And that's only if investigator took the time to ask the family or friends for these details.

Underground, investigators no longer have access to new clues. Nowhere is this more challenging to an investigator than the inability to extract previously uncollected DNA. It has only been in the past few decades that DNA collection has become more commonplace. Collection of DNA markers for scores of individuals across the country make up the groundwork for searchable databases. The most common are those collected by law enforcement seeking to solve crimes. But other prominent searchable websites also have DNA profiles entered for the benefit of genealogical tracing.

When family members—even distant family members—register their DNA in a database, investigators and families alike may be able to match DNA from an unknown person to their own family line with absolute certainty. Exhuming a body to look for a DNA sample, therefore, may have limited value if no familial DNA is on file somewhere.

Exhumations are infrequent and expensive. Spending thousands of dollars is pointless unless something inside a casket can be used to confirm a person's identity. That's what Michigan State Police (MSP) Trooper Sarah Krebs understood when, in 2013, she asked Leslie and her team to pull two bodies from a cemetery west of Detroit. Sarah's job is coordinating the state's missing persons program and includes looking for ways to match missing persons files with bodies found. Investigative leads on this occasion pointed to two buried bodies. She knows if she exhumes the bodies, the DNA might produce the genetic markers that will finally give her their identities. On this thankfully dry day, after her investigation shows a possible match, she obtains money to cover the expense of the two exhumations. She obtains a court ordered search warrant. She calls on Leslie's team to do the digging.

Arriving team members stand and wait for orders. Leslie's words are limited. To call in team members, she "tones" out for different types of assistance, avoiding the need to shout out names altogether or place a call to get someone to the site. Michigan is a busy crime state, so the team is experienced, and she never comes to a site unprepared. She understands what safety and other specialized equipment her team needs and has had it all pre-loaded in the team trucks. When they get to a crime scene, her team will draw sketches and take photographs as she decides how it will be searched.

Exhumations have their own challenges. Weather threatens the hours-long process. And, a burial degrades evidence quickly. Sarah has asked for Leslie's assistance because she knows her team has the best diggers in the state. Sarah's case has a Detroit nexus, and, for the first time, Shannon, on Sarah's invitation, is attending an exhumation. Standing on the sidelines at United Memorial, she watches as Leslie command her team. It's visible even from a distance. No one touches the site until Leslie walks it and decides who to bring in and when. Her movements are measured. Someone from her team is directed to begin sketches and another takes photographs.

Shannon had never met Leslie or her team. With equal parts squeamishness and intrigue, she watches as the team brings up long-buried body bags now filled with groundwater and a mix of bones and whatever might have been buried with the corpse.

Exhumations have their own smell, Shannon learns.

The forensic anthropologist who volunteered on scene reaches into the bag to try to find just the right bones in hopes of a DNA match. It takes a skilled hand to find the right bone, and forensic anthropologists study years to hone their craft. The "right bone" is one that might have enough material in it for a lab to find a DNA marker. Fingers, not so much. A single rib, negative. A femur. That's a big thick bone that might yield results. Another common bone to search for: ankle bones. Not every bone guarantees a good sample, so it's important to look for the right one among the 206 to 270 bones most humans have from birth to death. Babies have more, but they fuse together as they grow.

It might take months or possibly years to get the testing done, but locating DNA is a good start. In training, forensic anthropologists learn not only to identify what bones they are examining, but also what they see or feel that speaks to the age of the bone, or a determination of whether a damaged bone may have suffered a break from a violent act.

DNA is short for deoxyribonucleic acid, one of the components that can be detected in the cells of every living organism. It's a discovery attributed to Swiss physiological chemist Friedrich Miescher in the 1860s, followed by decades of research to help the science community comprehend how DNA and ribonucleic acid, or RNA, function to carry genetic information that can uniquely identify each person. Under the right microscope, a strand of RNA looks a bit like a corkscrew because of its helix shape. DNA, however, is more stable and has a familiar double helix shape with the two helixes intertwined. Its stability makes it easier to detect and obtain rather than RNA.

The discovery of the double-helix structure is credited to molecular biologists James Watson, an American, and Francis Crick, an Englishman, as well as to the work by English scientists Maurice Wilkins and Rosalind Franklin. The three men were awarded a Nobel Prize for their work in 1962, but Franklin was denied the Nobel, most likely because awards generally were not awarded posthumously. She had died of ovarian cancer four years earlier, in 1958. Her death, at the age of 37, was a cruel irony. She had been researching the molecular structure of viruses when she died, research that eventually earned her research partner the Nobel Prize in chemistry.

DNA research is the backbone of training now required for forensic anthropologists, and therefore students study the work of many other scientists who provided pieces to the genetic puzzle, including Russian biochemist Phoebus Levene, Austrian biochemist Erwin Chargaff, American biochemists Linus Pauling and Robert Corey, American scientist Jerry Donohue, and British scientist Raymond Gosling. It was Gosling, a student working for Franklin, who took the first successful image of the double helix, famously known as Image 51.

Research isn't just theoretical; it's a practical necessity. Long gone are the days when people were born, lived, and died in the same community. Global migration patterns through the centuries have mixed our human species, homo sapiens, with such a variety of ancestries that no one is definitively from a unique sub species, whether Asian, African, Native American, European, and Oceanian. We understand this because of landmark research performed by a team of global geneticists who worked from 1990 to 2013 to create a map of all the genes of our species–together known as the genome. The Human Genome Project was spearheaded by the U.S. National Institutes of Health, the largest biomedical research agency in the world, with support by the U.S. Department of Health and Human Services.

The project's result allows anyone worldwide to read nature's complete genetic blueprint for building a human being. Their results eclipsed old theories in the world of genetics and discussions about race, for example, were forever upended. The findings now aid the world's scientific community as it tries to better understand human health and disease. The Human Genome Project is ranked in importance to mankind alongside Einstein's Theory of Relativity and discoveries such as electricity and penicillin. It also opened the floodgates to scores of other scientific advancements.

Today, geneticists, anthropologists, and other scientists are trained to understand and identify the genetic "bar code," akin to a bar code found on a product in a grocery store. Trillions of DNA combinations exist, compared to the less than 10 billion people living on Earth, making identification of each individual possible. This type of identification also extends to relatives through family DNA samples. These scientific discoveries were helped with the understanding that every person acquires 50 percent of their DNA from each parent, for a total of 100 percent.

Researchers have determined with certainty that DNA can be tracked generation after generation, forward and backwards, when looking for familial DNA matches. A 50 percent match is perfect to connect two siblings, or a mother or father with a child. A 25 percent match indicates not just a grandchild, but also cousins and even another blood-related grandparent.

Scientific advances add on to one another, like rungs on a ladder. Each rung allows the next scientist to discover more, as they start from a better vantage point. It's the decades of these types of advances that Shannon hopes will eventually expand her ladder up to find the missing DNA and then up again to bring missing family members back together.

She digs her heels in metaphorically and determines that she will use DNA and anything else she can discover to forever change the way murdered victims are treated in Detroit.

CHAPTER 11

Who Am I, Where Am I, Here I Am

Running out of desk space, Shannon looks around until her eyes land on the tan fabric wall dividers beside her. Rising, she grabs a missing person flier and tacks it onto the cloth wall. That will do, she thinks, pleased with herself.

The newly missing are the most urgent pictures to display. Maybe this teen has only been gone a day or two. If they aren't found, maybe a body will show up and that's closure of one sort. She hopes to find that low hanging fruit and wants to keep information at the ready. She pulls open the top folder on the closest stack of files. She could post more. She picks up a missing person flier with a photo and approaches the wall.

This is working. She posts a few more fliers but then stops. Something is wrong. Some of these files are for missing people but others are files on dead people who have been found. She returns to her desk and opens a new blank document on her computer, typing *Where am I?* in 44-point, black, Times New Roman font. She hits print. Then she types *Who am I?* She heads to the printer.

She tacks the news signs in place at the top of the fabric wall, one on the left, one on the right. She relocates the right pictures and fliers under their proper headings. More fliers and pictures go up. As they grow in number, she smushes them together, overlapping the bottom half of a page with a new page. Among the files are kids whose parents disappeared and parents whose kids disappeared. It's working. She can already see how this will work to find matches. With the little excitement she musters, Shannon adds a third category, *Here I Am!*, to the wall. Now she has a spot to display and remind herself of her successes.

Each day the faces stare back at her.

In time, every inch of the soft-sided cubicle wall is filled from the top down to the floor and from the left edge to the right. She needs more room. Exasperated, she pulls all the *Who Am I?* papers over to the next wall divider. As the days go by, she expands from one wall panel to two, then three, then four. Still holding more photos and with no empty wall space remaining, she looks at her successes. These victories would have to be forgotten. She pulls down the *Here I Am!* matches. She stuffs them in file folders in the bottom of a desk drawer.

She's making progress. Yet, day after day, the faces stare back at her. The cases stubbornly refuse to migrate to the *Here I Am!* drawer and include dozens and dozens of cold case homicides. All the victims, perhaps more than she has space for, are listed as unidentified. Reports detail newborns found dead in a trash can and charred bodies and photos with the top of a head chopped off.

Those *Who Am I?* photos hang next to information on a man last seen on 8 Mile Road, a physical and psychological dividing line separating Detroit from the suburbs to the north. Shannon posts next to him a picture of a teenage girl who seems to have vanished from her own bedroom. Then, a photo of a man with only half a face. Was the other half blown off by a shotgun?

Each day, she sits silently with hundreds of grisly images and lost faces staring back at her. They deserve peace. She can practically hear them calling for her to give them peace. But the most challenging—Detroit's cold case homicides—are not getting solved. There wasn't enough evidence. They had no name. A few files have DNA from the victim, but the complex signature was a dead end. No matching family member DNA can be found in police or private databases. Unless someone steps forward with a new lead or a family member offers a DNA sample that matches, she is standing still. She had taken the missing person's desk to help families with the missing. Now, with the realization that cold cases were mixed in, she is needs to catch murderers.

She needs Sarah Krebs' help from the MSP. Tell me more about the Missing in Michigan program, she asks. Would the DNA program jump start her effort to put names to the murder victims? There are more than 100 cold case homicides, she tells Sarah. If a person has been missing a long time, an investigation could be reinvigorated if DNA could be matched to a family who could provide new information, and a fresh set of eyes could look at the known facts. She and Sarah begin more intense conversations.

If a person traveled or was taken out of town, the DNA sample could be particularly helpful, Sarah tells her, because there are several DNA databases and they exist without borders, making them international. Long missing people are found by families.

Sarah tells Shannon that MSP sets up tents at county fairs, job fairs, and government events and they are always looking for law enforcement to sit for the day and collect what they need. They encourage passersby to share information about the person missing, even if it has been a long time. If they can convince the person, Sarah says, they get a cheek swab. The swab of body fluid ideally provides extractable DNA. The DNA profile, more accurate than a fingerprint, then can be loaded into the growing database of civilian DNA managed by the FBI, and other private databases too.

She agrees to try in the spring. It has been three years since she started down this road and she still has one or two hundred unsolved homicide cases papering her wall. She's not even sure how many there are because the warehouse files are a mess and random people and notes from other officers keep getting dropped on her desk. So many have no good leads. Now would be a good time to set about matching her known DNA murder victims with a family member's DNA.

When the spring of 2016 opportunity arrives, she is there behind the school lunchroom table, hoping people will approach. She's not a chatterbox, so it's not her favorite spot to be. The day drones on with no takers, but a few who glance her way. She tries to smile.

One lone person stops, a 30-something year old named Antonio who reports a missing family member. She confesses that she doesn't know if a missing person file exists in police records. Tell me what you know, and I'll start a new investigation, she directs him, hoping not to fat finger her entries as she types on her laptop. She swabs his cheek and returns to her chair. Maybe she'll call it a day. She waits a bit longer. She has a lot of cases to clear. No one else stops by.

Shannon knows sometimes family members come by the station, looking for answers. But that's one of the things she hates. Sometimes she must tell families not that she doesn't have information on their loved one, but that she doesn't know if she does. She has all these unidentified murder victims in so many files she doesn't know if she has their loved one or not because she doesn't have the DNA samples to verify.

Some who stop by DPD about a missing family member do leave a DNA sample. They are told that after processing at a lab, their DNA can be checked to see if it matches DNA already listed in a relatively new federal Department of Justice database, or they can become the match that's missing. The database was set up specifically to help find the missing, whether through DNA or other evidence. But the DNA DPD is collecting rarely seem to hit on anyone in the DOJ database.

She knows if a person has been missing a long time, an investigation could be reinvigorated if the family provides new information. It's a fresh set of eyes to match with known facts. Some cases are being solved. But the most challenging—Detroit's cold case homicides—are not getting solved and few files include DNA on the victim. Unless someone steps forward with a new lead or a family member offers a DNA sample as a possible match, she is pretty sure they are out of luck on an identification, and out of luck on a chance to heal a family and, maybe, catch a murderer.

Her burgeoning spreadsheets are producing some fruit, at least in helping her understand the challenges of both finding the missing and finding the missing who were murdered. It's formidable. Nearly a dozen people are reported missing a day, every day. She calculates that of the 300 or so people who go missing in Detroit each year, about two-thirds of them are quickly recovered and identified. About half of those return home on their own or might not actually be missing. That leaves her with about 100 people truly missing each year, all of whom need to be tracked down individually.

So, who is truly missing? Some appear to have left the city voluntarily with no intention to return. Sometimes an elderly person who left was later found to be in a hospital. She is matching a couple dozen each year to someone who died, but the cause wasn't a police matter. Maybe they died from a drug overdose or old age. Many, though—particularly those missing for a long time—are likely homicide victims. That leaves Shannon having to decide on what cases she should spend her time.

She is fielding three or four calls every year where someone tells her somebody is buried on some land or in a building. But she can't just go out and dig someplace. Digging requires a search warrant or permission from a property owner. Maybe the information is bad. First, she has to do some vetting, see who lives on the property, how long the house has been there, if there are any facts to corroborate.

The most frustrating part is that the number of missing is increasing by 14 or 15 a year. To Shannon, that's 14 or 15 brothers, sisters, mothers, fathers, or children. She often repeats those words aloud. It's her go-to reality check on what she's trying to manage, even if she mostly grumbles it to herself. The pattern is the same throughout Michigan and in other states. When 2020 ended, there were 40 more children missing in Michigan who weren't missing at the year's start. Many of those were from Detroit and the disappearances happened on Shannon's watch.

She is drowning. She needs help to move people off the walls. She wants to work smarter, not just harder, but as she sits at her desk and the faces stare back at her, she is at a loss. Getting the details on a dead person is complicated.

Even when she has some basic information about a buried bone or body, her first moves are rudimentary. Sometimes pushing a probe into the site helps to determine if the ground has been disturbed or is too soft compared to the ground around. Occasionally, she has managed to get aerial views that highlight where the ground is visually different because it was dug up. Even when she is sure, she won't take a shovel out herself.

She doesn't really like working with other people. But, she argues with herself, digging and collecting evidence takes time and it can only be done right the first time.

After seeing Leslie's team at work, Shannon slowly begins to warm to the idea of working with the FBI. She knows her own evidence team at DPD is nothing to write home about. With one shot to do it right, she knows that the horrendous DPD team isn't her first choice for safely digging up a body or bones and preserving them to protect evidence for a criminal trial. She can't even think about them collecting and protecting potentially valuable DNA.

It is a monumental step to those who know her. Her comfort at remaining silent is so pronounced it makes those around her uncomfortable. Particularly since her divorce, the shell around her had grown thicker. When she marries again, it is to a kind firefighter who works different hours, and who is in his own world. Her front office leaves her alone and gives her time to think outside the box.

Shannon and Leslie's paths begin to cross more often, call after call. Sometimes bodies are buried in a yard or park. Other times bones are found in the water or when a building is being taken down.

"Shannon usually gets the case first," Leslie explains, "then calls me to consult on it. We both worked separately and developed our own skills without knowing each other. But we have also developed together over time on all the scenes we've worked. Once we get on a scene together, we fall in sync with each other. Very rarely do we disagree on the theory of crime or movement throughout the scene.

"I go on a lot of body searches and most of the time I can tell you the body isn't there quickly, but we still have to look," Leslie says. 'On those cases where we found the body it's a totally different feeling. When you're successful and experienced in the death investigation world, you develop that sixth sense."

A bit of a dirt whisperer, she can smell the dirt to see if they are close to human remains, which smell differently than animals. She describes how death has a unique sweet smell that hits you in the back of the throat. Shannon loves that Leslie's team is so technically trained and needs no instruction or help. And she also loves that they are free. Money is in short supply at DPD. There is nobody else that she could partner with, she admits in front of Leslie one day in her office. They understand the silence that follows. Neither needs a buddy at work. They need people who will do their jobs.

Shannon likes this silent partnership and decides the time is right to talk about an idea she has been brewing.

She calls Leslie, asking her to come by. Leslie is drawn to the horror that covers the walls, and asks the obvious—with a staid tone; "What's up with all these faces on here? It's creepy. Why do you have this?"

But Shannon is comfortable standing in her office. She is at home with the photos of bloodless bodies, disfigured images, and yellowed missing person reports tacked up nearby. Each represents an outstanding homicide or missing person, she says candidly. She is ready for bolder efforts.

She explains. The open missing persons cases date back to 1959. She begins as if she is showing off her family scrapbook. She estimates she is managing somewhere north of 250 open cases. Paper stolen from the copier room because it is more available than notepads are filled with handwritten notes about how a body or bone was found, where it was located, and whether it was burned or shot or otherwise. Graphic photographs of the missing hang near slips of paper with names, dates of birth, and onetime addresses.

Occasionally, she gets a call from a family member or another detective, she tells Leslie. But the technology at DPD "sucks," and putting the stuff up on the walls makes it easier to find things. Her impatience is showing. It is time to find DNA for anyone still up there, she says. She needs to connect those unnamed homicide victims with some DNA, so they all have names.

I'm tired of waiting for families to come forward, she complains to Leslie, pointing to all the photos and files surrounding her. I'm tired of having to wait for me to get that push where I can say "Okay, I think this person might be in the cemetery. Let's go out there and exhume this body."

Leslie waits. What is Shannon asking?

Detroit has hundreds of unidentified bodies in its paupers' graves in county cemeteries, Shannon explains. But no one in the seemingly always-near-bankrupt city of Detroit is paying for exhumations. MEs are busy concentrating on keeping up with the bodies coming in each day. They aren't in the business of identifying long deceased ones. Surely those bodies have detectible DNA, right, she says to Leslie in the form of a question without waiting for a reply.

Leslie is still perplexed. Frustrated, Shannon points to dozens of cold case murder victims. The files indicate they are all buried in pauper's graves in two cemeteries at the western edge of Wayne County.

Shannon persists. There are 298 unidentified buried bodies from Detroit going back to 1959. "I believe we have DNA on just a little over 100 of them," she explains to Leslie. "So instead of digging them up one by one, let's just dig them all up. If we dig them all up and take DNA samples," she explains, "no one will ever have to go back to the cemeteries again because now DPD is collecting DNA moving forward.

And, they can ask for DNA from family members looking for long-lost relatives."

Leslie's eyes widen with incredulity. Shannon is talking about 198 bodies. Repeating to be sure of what she is hearing, she asks, "What do you mean, dig them all up? "

Shannon realizes then that she is sounding ridiculous and slows down. The idea has been brewing in her head for a while.

Together they stand, looking at her walls of faces, bodies, and missing person fliers. Does it seem ridiculous, Shannon asks, gut checking her idea. She has no guarantee familial DNA is even available to match any of those bodies. Their fanciful goal is to put a name and face to the city's hundreds of unsolved homicides and missing person cases and try to solve the cold case murders once and for all.

Leslie is stunned. Maybe Shannon doesn't realize it, but she is asking Leslie to conduct the largest exhumation effort the FBI has ever undertaken. It will undoubtedly take years. Leslie thought back to her study of ancient Egypt. Everyone has read stories about solving a 100- or 200-year-old murder case. They read like a good mystery book. This isn't one body.

This will be different. If they start solving murders in more recent years—closing a cold case 15, 30, or even 50 years old—it becomes more than a good mystery book. The potential is evident immediately. Murderers might still be alive.

Family members might still be alive, Shannon says aloud, alert to the conversation Leslie is having inside her head.

"I do like to dig," Leslie says.

CHAPTER 12

What's Dead in the Forest?

Jodi Barta walks through a clearing and into the thick stand of trees. Any lingering indications something might have been buried beneath have disappeared. Jodi is a forensic anthropologist—the science of examining human skeletal remains, which includes assisting law enforcement investigations. She recognizes that their first task is the most onerous: simply finding the right place to dig.

Experts like Jodi rely on a virtual toolbox of indicators to help find something underground, including visible changes in vegetation and depressions and cracks in the ground surface. The first steps need to be quite rudimentary. The most useful option is a probe or soil coring tool. With a skilled hand, efforts to slip a probe into the ground can reveal subtle soil disturbances. If things go her way, she can detect a macabre clue. A probe pulled from the ground can smell a certain way if it has encountered a decomposing body.

Until the weather improves, her priority is to protect the area from curiosity seekers and hungry animals. She looks for any sign of trouble. Michigan winters can be long and cold, and the state's more than 11,000 lakes keep the humidity high, adding to the chill in the often-bitter cold. Once the ground thaws, the work can begin in earnest.

Come on spring.

Before probing, searchers do a visual inspection. The ground cannot completely hide visitors. When someone buries something—like a body—no amount of dirt tamped on the disturbed ground will be enough to prevent what soon will be a settling of the earth. Someone who has walked over the area may break sticks or drop items as they leave. If their suspicions are correct and a burial site is found under those trees, she explains to her crew, then they will cordon off the area and begin the process of slow, methodical steps needed to look for human remains.

Anxious to see whether a body is buried in the woods, they head to the site at the first sign of spring. First, she explains to the team, they need photographs. Searches in support of potential criminal cases always begin with photos to document what the scene looked like before it was disturbed. Juries like photos and have come to expect them.

Cautiously, her team gathers at the edge of the site, anxious for their assignments. Some shift and sway, distracted by the cold. Jodi explains the steps. It's methodical and each step has a purpose. She dispatches a photographer and then assigns another to begin sketching out the site.

Touching her probe to the ground, she detects the uneven depression as the soil settled over time. She explains what loamy soil looks like to her, sort of lumpy, and describes how it gives way more easily in ever so slight ways as she pushes the probe into the ground. This is an indication the ground has been disturbed. She hands the probe to one team member and then another to try.

If work with a probe detects loamier soil, she explains, that may indicate something is there. She directs them to move to the next step and assigns a few to string a grid over the whole area where the ground appears to have been disturbed. They set the grid with wooden stakes and string, designating letters up one side and numbers down the next. This bingo-card system of locators will give searchers a quick and easily identifiable square to use as a point of reference for anything found on or under the soil.

This pattern of small uniform squares makes it easier for forensic anthropologists and law enforcement investigators to piece together a visual of what lies below, even recreating it above ground in their laboratories, as necessary. She knows that sometimes bodies or skeletons are found intact. But at other times bones found may indicate the site could have been disturbed by an animal or there may be evidence of a homicide, such as the partial or full dismemberment of the victim. Document as you go is the rule. You only get one chance to collect the evidence the right way.

While sketching is underway, she turns to others. Let's get this screening area set up nearby, she says. A folding table is best because the searchers will bring anything they find to the table, identifying the bingo square of origin. Sieves and brushes in the dig kit help distinguish evidence from dirt and rocks, and sticks and leaves.

She gathers the team. In dig sights, she explains, it may be more difficult to find every potential piece of bone or bone fracture. Items overlooked are missed clues for investigators. Pieces of fabric, buttons, and anything that might not belong below ground naturally should be bagged and tagged. To combat this challenge, she says, a simple screen sieve ensures every possible item that might be found can be. It's like holding a very fine window screen horizontally, so when it is shaken gently, the dirt can fall below while items remaining on the screen can be picked through.

She knows this is especially important when investigators are faced with a large volume of debris and looking for even the tiniest pieces of bone and other human matter. She knew similar screens were tacked on a conveyor belt in 2001 when hundreds of searchers sifted through the post-9/11 debris from the fallen Twin Towers. The process is slow, Jodi explains to the team, but it's the only way to learn how to properly dig up a body and other potential pieces of evidence. With each item found, she has another team member mark an evidence bag with the grid location and pop the item inside. Paper bags tend to keep the evidence best protected for transport. Plastic can trap moisture and speed up degradation.

Within hours, the entire site has been searched and all the evidence collected. Her spring ritual of having her students dig up a body has been successful, if a bit unorthodox. Telling is instructive, but doing is so much more valuable, she tells her dig team, all students in one of her classes. Jodi is the chairman of the Forensic Science Department at Madonna University in Livonia, about 20 miles due west of Detroit.

Jodi spent a decade creating and developing the state's first accredited forensic science undergraduate program certified by the Forensic Science Education Programs Accreditation Commission. Her route to Madonna was as unpredictable as her life. But once there, she had taken science classes designed for an impressive nursing program and built on them to create a first-of-its kind program where graduates could go into a variety of related fields.

About 2,500 students attend the private Catholic university, founded in 1937. Jodi's labs and office space spread out over the west side of the building, hidden behind the red brick, two-story Franciscan Center. In the hallway, a glass wall case announces the Forensic Science Research Facility and displays a copy of true crime author Earl James' book, *Catching Serial Killers*, as well as the latest *Journal of Forensic Identification*. Beside them, a human skull and other bones. Yellow crime scene tape frames the display that shows off a plaster cast of a footprint, likely taken from a crime scene.

Gray bulletin boards blanket the industrial tan hallway walls, each covered in oversize posters of successful projects by faculty and staff. Tacked on the wall outside Jodi's teaching lab, the first one reads: "Answering Question of Social History Using Ancient DNA to Analyze Skeletal Remains from the Spring Street Presbyterian Church Cemetery, New York." Jodi is one of the authors.

In her office, nearly every inch of available space is filled, unexpectedly, in great part with whimsy. One or two family photos can be found. Paper skeletons from the Halloween aisle hang from bookshelves crammed with textbook titles on anatomy and physiology beside twenty or so more titles that include the word genetic. (Analysis, Genetic Essentials, Introduction to Genetic Analysis). Stacked on top of the books and surrounding every other available space are binders of research projects and copies of Madonna University manuals on safety and other policies. Photos of her working in the lab and Christmas cards from her students remain, ignoring the seasons that have passed.

Her impatience and sense of humor are reflected in the artifacts. A coffee mug that boasts: "I survived another meeting that should have been an email." A peek at her personal history—the parts she knows—are hidden on the shelves by the window; a photo with two adult kids and a handful of toys adorned with the maple leaf flag of her homeland, Canada.

Clipped to a magnet and affixed to the side of a metal bookshelf by the light switch, a sign reads: "I have three sides: 1. The little quite sweet side 2. The fun and crazy side 3. The side you never want to see." The tattered paper sign hangs next to other items that few likely would appreciate—an empty Twix candy bar and a crumpled Skittles bag.

Nearly a third of Madonna's students are female and she knows most will graduate and go on to medical, dental, or pharmacy school, or work in any number of forensic areas, including forensic anthropology and DNA analysis. Their tasks might include ammunition evaluation, detecting evidence of homicides, and securing latent fingerprints.

She is obsessive and exudes impatience that overwhelms some. Ultimately, she wants students to know how to use their specialized talents to examine the bodies of those who may have been murdered but never identified. That translates into excessive hours working with students and hours staging elaborate dig sights and taking students out of the classroom to real dig sites. Students describe her in Rate My Professor in glowing and condemning terms. "Genetics is an intense course, but the payoff is worth it," one wrote. One offers, "She doesn't coddle you. She expects you to use your brain." A third condemns, "Can get snippy when not following her directions." She's used to it. She knows that life is tough and it's better to ignore the negative people.

Theory meets practice when she hands students real police files. It's a chance for her students to review the cold case homicides and talk about the photos and evidence within. You can turn a cold case into a solved murder, she tells them.

Students review real files from unsolved cases provided by the local police and discuss details from the original files. Consider what investigators may have missed, neglected, or even purposefully ignored, she says. Were there opportunities to gather more evidence that could lead to the identify of an unidentified body?

After discussing what might be in an autopsy, she asks, what is the purpose of an autopsy? Yes, she agrees, to establish cause of death. But should an autopsy be done on every dead person? Students disagree. They aren't always done, their professor explains. People under a doctor's care in a hospital have declarations from the doctor of the cause of death. People in car accidents may have obvious and severe trauma that explains the death. Other families refuse to allow an autopsy to be performed for religious or other reasons.

This day, Jodi wants to focus their conversation on the unsolved homicides, the cold case files where police do not know the identity of the victim. Anytime an unidentified person is going to be buried an autopsy should include whatever police can gather. What will that include? She asks. Photographs, fingerprints, dental records, DNA, they offer. Also, personal items, she notes. Clothing, jewelry, contents of pockets, and things found with them.

But looking at the files, students share what's missing. Some don't have pictures. Others have no dental records. Why is a body buried, in a pauper's grave with no dental images preserved, she asks them rhetorically. She expresses frustration at the sloppy work in some of the files. Look at how many items are missing in this autopsy, she says. Look at how few details are in the police report.

Her students are young and likely don't remember a time when DNA wasn't around. They are learning to extract DNA using all the equipment around them. But she knows not every student will graduate and take a job in a lab and she wants them to appreciate the entire investigative process. DNA isn't necessary if a dental match works, she tells the class. She encourages her students to consider other ways a murder could be solved.

This is why each fall, when the students aren't around, she shows up with her box of surprises. Assuring there are no onlookers, she moves within the forest adjacent to the school. She is careful not to break newly sprouting trees or small branches that would give away her final location choice. Forensic anthropologists don't usually lead a dig—they are called in to do the surgical work, the kind of work only they can do. But learning the entire process is invaluable to future job opportunities, as well as helping them to fully appreciate the scope of an investigation.

When she goes to set the stage, she carefully lifts and sets aside bigger branches and a few rocks. Next, the leaves. The leaves need to be pushed aside, but not buried. These things all need to be replaced, just as if an actual murderer had been there. Her site choice must take on some practical considerations. If she's too good, they may lose a day or two just looking for the disturbed site. Digging too deep could be bad, but digging too shallow might mean that the site does not survive Michigan's winter weather conditions, or a visiting raccoon, deer, or even a curious kid.

The site needs to have the evidence spread far enough apart to allow students to practice digging and dusting and sifting, but not so far apart that pieces of a victim or evidence from the victim are never found. That's the fun part of the job. As she carefully places each piece of "evidence," she needs to make a detailed map for herself. Though she has her own epic tale of memory loss, she needs good notes to make sure nothing is forgotten here. She concentrates on what-was-buried-where. It's good not to forget as fall turns to winter turns to spring.

She likes unearthing the buried "body" in the campus forest each spring because it teaches students how to do it, not just to study the process. She tells them that while police might be able to dig up a body, only a skilled forensic anthropologist can reach into a bag of bones and, with near certainty, identify which of the couple hundred bones they have picked up.

Their pristine labs contrast with the condition of her office. You could eat lunch on the table save for the reality of the location. That's driven home when she pulls out a blue-capped, clear 28-by-26-inch plastic bin. A piece of masking tape is affixed to the side reads "Tibiae & Fibulae." Inside, about two dozen bones of various sizes and characteristics have been carefully placed on bubble wrap lining the bottom and sides.

The wall shelves have a handful of similar bins with different bones, so the students can analyze each. "This one is a right fibula," she says to her students, holding it up. Another shows evidence the bone was damaged after the person was dead. The calcification on another helps a future expert estimate the age of the person at the time of death.

The most important tools for forensic anthropologists are your hands and eyes, she says. Her goal is to have students be comfortable helping police identify whether something is a human bone, its potential characteristics, and then, whether that bone may have suffered trauma before death.

Her lab space is blanketed with items efficiently stored for quick access. Glass and plastic containers cover the counters and are filled with local lake water, acids, solutions, and a variety of reagents used to draw more information from the bones. Each is an opportunity to learn to analyze a bone that is found. Medical equipment and other tools of the trade cover countertops and spill into an adjoining storage room with shelves meticulously organized and where everything has a sign on it identifying whether the box content is sterilized or unsterilized. White student lab coats stacked on top of each other hang onto the three little plastic hooks that have been affixed to the end of the line of eight-foot-tall shelving units.

A human skeleton hangs by the door. DNA model kits sit on the shelf of her adjoining classroom, which is lined with chalkboards. The functional metal white tabletops include sinks. A necessity in such a workspace. This work can get messy.

There is no room for whimsy here.

On television and in the movies, forensics is falsely absolute and always quick. Early on, the main characters look at the half-buried bones of a skeleton and say into the camera, "this man was murdered," she says with a bit of disdain, appreciating that the declaration moves the plot along. I want scratch and sniff television, she tells the students, and for directors not to film people bending over a body with no masks and no suits on.

"You know those things are covered with maggots that jump," she says. "They never show that."

CHAPTER 13

Listening to Bones

In class, Jodi's students learn more than book knowledge of biology and anthropology. She is teaching them to listen to what the bones reveal and to hear the bones. Was this bone injured when the person was alive and were the wounds older and had time to heal? Was a body likely cut up or damaged after a person died? How old are the bones? Subtle changes identified may reflect phenotypic, or observable, characteristics from centuries of humans adapting to certain climates, geographic locations, diet, or even the physical demands of survival.

A full skeleton or even a partial can tell a forensic anthropologist much more. Jaws, teeth, and facial construction can disclose age ranges and even more amorphic categories, such as characteristics that might give clues to race and gender. From a science standpoint, she explains, the latter are just educated guesses since race and gender are societal, not biological categories.

"There are five sexes. We have female, we have metafemale, we have intersex, we have meta male, and we have males," she tells them in class. "This is very confusing for people who are stuck in a binary world. But as an educator, I need people to understand that this is a biological certainty; biological, not lifestyle."

Decades of repeated scientific research has validated that biological characteristics vary beyond the two-sex, binary world that lives on standardized government and so many other everyday forms. But for centuries, societies have varied in the way they construct gender roles ascribed to females, males, and gender-diverse people. Social constructs can mislead investigators, but not forensic anthropologists. Social constructs have relied on external and internal genitalia, chromosome testing, and hormone levels. None are true proxies for biological sex, she says.

Forensic scientists learn all of this to prevent them from jumping to what could be inaccurate conclusions as they work, she explains to her students. At death, categories such as race, economic class, ethnicity, and even gender are permanently stripped away. Genetics is more complicated than what the uninformed often want it to be. Only society categorizes people as Black, White, European, or Asian American.

"I'm a geneticist," she explains. "It's important to understand that in genetics there's no such thing as race, because race is a social construct."

That is especially important in law enforcement because the first thing investigators often asks her is "What race was this person?"

"Well, you know that race doesn't exist, but what they're really asking is for phenotypic characteristics that will help to identify somebody," she says, explaining that these are the outwardly visible characteristic that have developed because of a person's environment. It's the reason the skin on the feet and hands is tougher and how that grizzled old sea captain earned his wrinkles and leathery skin.

Generations of people who have lived where the sun is most intense develop darker skin by increasing melatonin in their skin pigment to protect them from damaging ultraviolent sun rays.

"I'm the person that gets them when they're skeletons," Jodi laments, "Bones are all the same color, white."

After the results of the Human Genome Project were released, DNA catapulted to the top of desired evidence. The results changed everything for a world hungry to identify the anonymous. And for Jodi and her students, it enlightens their understanding of priorities. Though all their training is important, Jodi knows they also need to be proficient with the tens of thousands of dollars' worth of DNA testing equipment in Madonna's laboratories. Maybe one of them would change the world around them, one test at a time.

With every person getting 50 percent of their DNA from each parent, it's a certainty that a person who has a 25 percent DNA match is either a blood-related grandchild, grandparent, or cousin.

In a world where everyone focuses on scoring 100 percent, she said, it's important to erase from your mind the number as being like the odds in horse racing or lottery tickets. "Twenty five percent, that's really, really close because it's not a chance," she says, "it's a sharing of 25 percent of your DNA." Understanding this helps explain why trouble brews when people too closely related by blood have children of their own. One needs to look no further than the impact to European monarchies seeking to protect their blood line, she explains. That's why people went mad; it's Darwin's postulates at play.

Jodi's love for her students is a mixture of tough love and believing more than they do that they will be successful and can change the world. Her students learn that at the end of the day, when things become too genetically intertwined and harmful, the organism becomes sterile. For example, in the 17th century, the Spanish Empire lost its direct royal bloodline when King Charles II of Spain was the only surviving child of his mother's 11 children. He was born malformed and surely sterile, she said.

She shows them, with some pride, an excellent figure that delineates how King Charles II of Spain was more closely inbred than if his parents had been brother and sister. Genetic history lessons are fun, but Jodi loves to give her students opportunities for hands-on experience. That why reviewing police files and helping on digs is so valuable. She has clocked many hours with the Ontario Provincial Police and the Hamilton, Ontario Major Crimes Unit from her native Canada. Her bone picker role has placed her in the middle of cases and exhumations for years. Sometimes it's for the local police, sometimes state, sometimes the Feds, and sometimes for those organizations who just pursue missing persons.

Jodi knows the local FBI agent in charge of digs. They met when Leslie showed up with a femur bone that needed a home. Police investigators in Texas had determined that the bone belonged to a man who died in Texas but was originally from Detroit. He wasn't a good person, Leslie told Jodi, but the man's sister has contacted her asking, can you do something with this so that he could be of use in death, though he was not in life. Could you use the bone in the classroom, Leslie asked, which she received a quick yes. It was a great resting place for a not so nice person.

Working with police is an opportunity to create a well-rounded program and so she builds time for them to get out of the classroom. Her curriculum includes working with the Michigan State Police and several local police departments, particularly Detroit. To help police solve a homicide, she tells them, you need to understand police work and police files first. Your value isn't just as a forensic anthropologist, but also as an outsider.

An officer's implicit biases may result in an investigator assuming someone is a runaway or street person, prompting them to do little follow investigation. She's seen this in cases involving those victims who are historically marginalized and underprivileged.

Because of such established views about race in the US, Jodi finds it particularly important to have her students explore mistaken assumptions. Sometimes the toughest case may be unsolved because investigators' perceptions are clouded by false assumptions made about the victims, she says.

"They may see a Black teenager and say, probably involved in gangs, probably doing this, probably doing that, probably ran away, blah blah blah blah blah," she says mimicking what she's seen in the files. "In exactly the same way as, 'Oh, that teenager is engaging in prostitution, she's a prostitute, let's charge HER.'"

Look at the files with a critical eye, she says. You can tell by the questions asked, and the work done—or more importantly, not done—if assumptions might have been drawn because of the race of the body found. And it's not just about race, it's also reflected in the way cases are handled involving women, those socioeconomically challenged, the "lesser classes."

"Historically, there has been a hierarchy of value put on human lives, particularly in law enforcement," she explains. It's a classic narrative often applied to those who police encounter. Forensic anthropologists seemed to have earned their minor degrees in the skill of explaining this to the masses.

Wayne State University's Dr. Jaymelee Kim, who also would eventually join Shannon's efforts, explained to *The Fall Line* podcast audience, that even though ME records might identify three people as #1, #2, and #3, the cemetery workers might put them into the ground in a completely random way, leaving no way to tell the three males apart if they were buried on the same day. This carelessness reflects the value given to the marginalized in society, she says. "We have policies, law and practices embedded in our culture to keep the marginalized, marginalized."

Kim, and Western Michigan University's Dr. Carolyn Isaac, have joined forces to work on mass genocide and disaster sites in other parts of the word. They also help out Shannon and Leslie. "It's easy to think of this as a problem other countries face, but the truth is that there are so many in our own back yard, Isaac tells *The Fall Line*. "There are so many mistreated in life, who lose their identity in death."

Jodi knows her students are likely to encounter so many in their professional careers. The case files they are looking at, she points out, can telegraph neglect and disregard for others.

"When we're reviewing the old case files, we look at the interviewers and the questions they ask," she says. "You can literally tell what they already had in their mind, what had happened. They're in the middle of shoving everything that's said into their narrative that they've already formed.

"That's not to say that men are not empathetic," she points out, hoping not to discourage the male students. "But there are narratives that have been going on for a very, very long time in law enforcement, in the same way that you would charge a 17-year-old girl with prostitution and let the John go. Those are trafficked victims, but the narrative for so long has been one way."

She has worked with many investigative agencies and police departments. Perhaps that was why, in what seems her wise old owl style, she began to realize requests for her assistance from police were often from women and women-led teams. She had met these Michigan women on various investigations along the way as they developed a web of experts now operating full bore to identify homicide victims by using forensic anthropology, legal tools, and old-fashioned gumshoe investigative work.

She finds women bring additional skills to their jobs, a humanity honed by their cultural upbringing. Women often are placed in the role of peacemaker, fixer, and caretaker. They are more likely to bring those skills with them when they arrive at the office.

That's how women are, she says; they see something, and they get it done. They are willing to take on seemingly insurmountable challenges and work until they fix the problem. She wants her students to work with those women in law enforcement for this reason.

Jodi has worked with so many of them. Shannon and Leslie, and the other forensic anthropologists, including the women who run the body farms, are all women working on the most challenging cases. When she needed a prosecutor for the search warrant, Shannon turned to LaDonna, ready to step in and commit to the workload needed to dig up a couple hundred bodies from the cemeteries.

"I think that Shannon and Leslie especially, are very aware, being women in law enforcement, of the narratives, and some of the goals,"

Jodi explains during a class break. They recognize there can be a disproportionate impact on people of color, women, and the marginalized that impacts a disproportionate number of those who are murdered and who are buried in those pauper's graves.

"It's an awareness of the narrative that men in law enforcement just don't, or maybe can't understand, whether it be color, background, socioeconomic status, all of those things, or past drug use," she says. "It's exactly the same as somebody saying all lives matter. Yeah, no, duh. But White lives have always mattered. That's not the question, right? They're trying to tell you that Black lives also matter.

"We have to change that narrative and start to really think about the value of these women and girls who have gone missing, and the ones that were put into places like these cemeteries without being identified.

"As women, we do understand the narrative," she says, because women have historically been part of the lesser classes. "We are not happy with it, but often men, men don't even recognize it. That's the beauty of privilege, because privilege is when you think of something as a problem only if it's a problem for you."

Helping her students appreciate what was considered the standard in past decades is a way to better appreciate how assumptions about victims have occurred. Imagine the societal pressure for police to look for a missing White cheerleader whose dad is the bank manager, compared to the deafening silence of public outcry for a missing indigent child of a single Black mother working in a grocery. It begins with the false narrative about why these people ended up on the street. It's so evident when the assisting forensic anthropologists, MEs, and coroners review files. Those groups too, historically male, may make the same assumptions law enforcement makes, and the file discloses that. "It's an insulting and veiled disguise to diminish the life lost," she adds with disdain in her voice.

"I don't want to shit all over law enforcement," she says. "I really don't, but we have a framework within law enforcement that follows this might-is-right philosophy. I'm the authority; I tell you what's right. We need to critically think about what the value of human life is, and the factors that contribute to this hierarchy where one life is more valued over another. The disparities that these people suffered through during their lifetimes breaks my heart."

She appreciates how a life can simply disappear. She is compelled to stop that where she can. So, when Leslie and Shannon called, the answer seemed obvious. Could she and her students join in as the FBI begins its largest ever exhumation of a couple hundred bodies? Would she join the DPD and the FBI in what is likely the country's most ambitious effort ever attempted to clear hundreds of cold case murders—all at the same time?

In her mind, she is already reaching for her gloves and boots.

CHAPTER 14

Paper Caskets

Shannon telegraphs isolation with her downward and far-off gaze. To talk to her seems as if you are disturbing her more important thoughts. She is isolated and isolating. Putting the right team together will force Shannon to step outside herself.

Leslie, too, prefers her emotions be parked in the remote parking lot. She is painfully private until she knows you well. She dated as a younger FBI employee in Milwaukee, but rarely shared with her colleagues her preference for women over men. Law enforcement is a judgmental group.

She eschews see-saw emotions, a childhood characteristic validated by years in an ambulance and navigating evidence collection of murdered children or body parts of a victim blown apart by an explosion or a semi-automatic weapon's fire.

Leslie's demand for action over words matches Shannon's. They understand, Leslie more than Shannon, that at times they need to project the facade of warmth and confidence for the public or their team. Both would prefer to be sitting alone in their own cars.

"No screwing around," Shannon says to Leslie. "We're coming here to get this done, and that's it. We don't have time to talk."

No small talk.

To understand what she's about to tackle, Leslie joins Shannon at the Wayne County warehouse to survey the old homicide files that are gathering dust and taking up space. The warehouse stores police files, but also boxes of paper for several county offices-- zoning, building, licensing. It is a maze of once-important items now in varying states of disrepair. The former grocery has a high ceiling and file boxes are, at times, out of reach. Without a map, who would know where to look? It's not as complicated for Shannon. She's been there plenty of times.

Though they are rarely touched, each police file has the essential information, the trunk of the tree when it comes to seeing every other aspect of the cold case: who found the body, where it was found, its condition, and what was done to solve the murder. Some might think a 50-year-old case can't be solved, but Shannon explains how it can. She pulls out a file to show Leslie how to determine if they are even looking at a cold case homicide for an unknown person, aware the files are mixed in with other old police files. The layered information within is discernable only if you know what to look for among the papers.

Each body generates a single file, a paper casket. The worn and flimsy manilla cardboard carries all the remaining information about the life of an auto worker, a student, a runaway teen, a homeless veteran. Each is selfishly slight in detail. Investigators sometimes used the files as scratch paper, leaving notes written on the inside and outside of the jacket. Whether in pencil or pen, the hand scribbled notes are smeared in time and faded sheets of mimeographed paper once handled with care are folded and stuffed carelessly within. Some of the paper content leans towards unintelligible or simply undecipherable. Who wrote "B-1" on the top of that report and why does "645" appear on the top of another page? What do they mean?

The letters "ed" are handwritten in behind the description of a dead baby's "color" so that the identity is listed as "color-ed."

Shannon explains that all the files have one thing in common: An ME's determination that violence ended the life of the still unidentified person. Some files describe the clothes and personal items buried with the body. Most critical is a declaration of how the person was murdered. One or two paper doll-type drawings are included. The ME had hand marked Xs and circles to represent the location of bullet holes and spots where a person was shot, stabbed, or bludgeoned to death. Some files include photographs that slap the viewer with reality. Half of a face on a skull. Dismembered body parts sitting in a recreated body frame. Where most of a body is found, Shannon and Leslie look at an expressionless face lying on a cold metal table. The dead files paint a vivid picture of a city's transformation from hopeful to helpless.

She's been working missing persons for a few years now and she knows the routine. One-by-one, she explains, she has been bringing files of the unsolved murders to her office to see if she can tie an identity to the person or at least take additional investigative steps. Shannon is methodical. It's just a matter of going through the steps to pick out the files on the bodies they might be able to find in a dig, she tells Leslie. Ones that have the best hope of securing the prized DNA.

Once the file comes to her desk from the warehouse, she adds details to the spreadsheet. Pulling these first details, she searches electronic files and looks for matching information. Something in a file might tie the dead person to somewhere else. If she needs to reach out to other local police departments, she does. Maybe the body was found on the border of a neighboring town. Maybe there is something with value found on the body that no one followed up on. She cross checks the old files with newer information in Detroit's databases. Someone they thought was missing may no longer be missing.

She realizes that, through the years, an egregious and systematic error occurred that impacted all the cases. Maybe error isn't the right word. Maybe it's an omission or just a disregard grounded in the calamitous reality of the city's historic policies.

Detroit did not enter missing persons into any electronic database prior to 2010. Families may think there is a report on a missing person, a file that is being worked, but Shannon knows there is not. Detroit is likely not the only city with this problem, but Shannon often feels as if it is. If a potential lead comes into headquarters about a missing person, there is little they can do. More often than she would like to admit, people think there is an open case if they reported someone missing years before. But the reality is that no one is looking for that person. Police don't even have anything about them in a database.

"If we didn't have the electronic report or it may have been a report that was taken away, finding those missing person reports that were handwritten but are still in good condition has proven to be difficult at times," she says diplomatically.

How many paper files are there related to cold case homicides and missing person? No one has kept track. They are mixed in with the many other jackets of police activity. By Shannon's calculations, that's the problem for 200 to 300 cases. Searching paper files is laborious and often relegated to the last item on an investigator's to-do list. Her solution every time has been to simply create a whole new missing person's report.

As Leslie and Shannon spend more time together, flashes of respectful humor emerge.

It was a crazy idea from the start, Leslie explains when she knows Shannon is within earshot. She is quick to goad Shannon with a slightly different version of the plan they are developing.

"She's like, 'What if we do that 350 times or something?' I'm like, 'What do you mean 350?' She's like, 'I have 350 missing persons files,' and I'm like, 'I can't dig (up) 300 bodies in one day! What are you talking about?'"

"No," Shannon counters. "What if we just take a bunch of them? We'll just go, you and me and the team, we'll just go dig 'em up and see what happens."

Her idea for digging up a couple hundred bodies requires a good plan, and Leslie thrives on detailed plans. She devises a remarkably thorough and unexpectedly practical plan. Her teams can't just dig up two or three hundred bodies at once. But they can do it over a series of years. If they set about categorizing all the information they can from the files, adding what they locate in any current files, then a list of possible bodies to dig should become visible.

They move to the next phase, comparing the information from the police files with cemetery records. Shannon pulls a file. If it's a missing person's report from a specific day, month and year, she first looks to see if a person around the same age and sex was buried in the succeeding weeks or months.

Looking for one person seems like a longshot. She's not finding a lot of perfect matches. But she finds one, and then another. As she hoped, looking at hundreds of pieces of information all at the same time is providing a more sophisticated analysis. Excitedly, she moves forward. She just needs to keep plowing through the files.

It's a plan.

CHAPTER 15

Operation UNITED

Now the work begins. Who should they dig for first? When should they dig? Where should they dig in the cemetery? If they need to dig several times each summer, they will. What if it takes longer than they think?

Maybe it will be years, Shannon says, but her goal is to have it all done when she retires. She's starting the project less than a decade before retirement. The more potential matching information there is, the better. She reasons that as potential matches of files to cemetery plots multiply, they should be able to better strategize. She'll call this Operation UNITED, short for Unknown Names Identified Through Exhumation and DNA.

Shannon assures Leslie that if the FBI team leads the digs, they can tap into a DOJ National Institute for Justice (NIJ) program run through the University of North Texas (UNT) to get the expensive DNA testing done. DOJ funding allows the university to perform forensic genetic and anthropological examinations for criminal casework and missing persons identification and taps into operational databases that enable state and local crime laboratories to exchange and compare DNA profiles electronically in criminal cases.

"I can send my bones down there," she says. The university is home to the Center for Human Identification (UNT CHI), which provides screening and DNA testing services of biological evidence related to criminal investigations. Other agencies and organizations also submit DNA identification requests.

They begin to work through Leslie's logical and practical challenges. Besides freeing up her own team, she'll needs to ask FBI Headquarters for more supplies, and if she wants to bring in evidence team members from other FBI divisions, she'll need travel money. Headquarters is notoriously tight at budget time. She knows some teams around the country have people quite skilled in forensics and body recovery. If every big town has this problem, FBIHQ's criminal division is not going to be excited about wanting to pay to fly teams from all over the country just to help Detroit. But she needs the best the FBI has to offer.

Ignoring her proclivity to only chug energy drinks for sustenance, Shannon begins lunching occasionally with Leslie and the team. BJ's Restaurant & Brewhouse in Livonia is not far from Leslie's house. It's their favorite haunt.

The conversations are not for the faint of heart. Shannon's stories often begin with something like "so we fished" this body part or this guy from the Detroit River. There's the story about opening a series of Coleman coolers only to come face-to-face with dozens of facial skin masks staring back at her that had been peeled off skulls. There was the time Leslie made ERT members from another FBI division use a broom handle to swirl the content of a few 55-gallon barrels filled with liquid in a successful effort to coax numerous skulls to pop up to the top so they could be fished out, bagged, and tagged.

The stories are endless. Leslie's can be brutal. Over a sandwich and fries, she discusses pulling foot bones out from inside hundreds of shoes removed from the World Trade Center site. There's the time Leslie's team had to wait until a bitterly cold week in winter so they could commandeer a parking lot, mark it out with a rope in a grid pattern, and empty out hundreds of body parts being stored in refrigerator trailers so they could walk around and find a way to put as many people back together as they could, as if they were giant paper dolls whose legs, knees, feet, hands, elbows, arms, and heads had been accidentally scattered in a windstorm. It allowed the return of bodies to families.

In this business, you laugh so you don't cry. They are careful to keep their volume low to limit what the people at the nearby lunch tables hear. The other patrons are free to interpret what they want from the visible cringes and mixture of macabre laughter coming from the dark wooden table in the back corner of the Livonia eatery.

West of Livonia, they stop by the offices at the cemeteries where they know the homicide victims are buried in paupers' graves. Families who bury loved ones often like to pick out a sunny hill or a place under a tree where they can come and sit on a nearby bench to carry on a changed relationship with their loved one. But no one is coming to these paupers' graves, and no one has picked out an idyllic spot. They often are laid to rest with others who are known, but buried at the county's expense for any number of reasons.

Initially, homicide victims were all buried in Knollwood's, 40-acre park on what was once farmland in Canton Township. Its modest size makes it viewable nearly end to end.

Later, burials took place at United Memorial so far west you're closer to Ann Arbor. Each has its own atmosphere. Knollwood is on the curve of a county road and its small sign makes it easy to miss. United Memorial abuts a main state route, M-15, which could be mistaken for a federal interstate. Wide traffic lanes and a 100-foot median are cordoned off by wide shoulders that drop down into deep swales protected by a fence line.

Leslie sees the sites differently. Winter snow and all its salt and debris are plowed off the shoulder, threatening to bury the graves at the fence line of United Memorial. At the very least, the swale likely will often be full of melting snow and rainwater. The land settles and the far back corner has a visibly higher water table.

If Leslie can get her people there, Shannon will need to justify the time and expense of Operation UNITED to her command staff, including the reason why the cash poor city should divert resources away from current case work. But she needs this win. She realizes a lot of people will need to work for free or get their office to let them work on their own time.

Before an excavator scrapes grass from any burial site, Shannon's A-team is pulling the ME's notes. Interpreting the notations on the files is a task for Megan Moore from the Wayne County ME's office. Several forensic anthropologists will have to agree to be available on the three weeks each summer that they will dig. The FBI's Los Angeles-based Intelligence Analyst, Meredith Killough, can help. She is a forensic anthropologist who joined the FBI to become an agent. Jodi signs on, as do the all the female forensic anthropologists, including Jane, the Director of Northern Michigan University's FROST Center.

That first exhumation Shannon saw had cost thousands and was funded for the Michigan State Police by the National Center for Missing and Exploited Children or NCMEC, a private, not-for-profit corporation. Often referred to as "nick-mek" by those working kid-related cases, it serves as a clearinghouse for all things involving missing children. NCMEC trains volunteer investigators—mostly retired law enforcement.

The not-for-profit was born of the persistent effort of co-founders John Walsh and his wife, Revé Drew Walsh, and a handful of other advocates. The couple's son, Adam, was abducted from a Sears department store in Hollywood, Florida in 1981. A long, ongoing media frenzy ended when Adam was found murdered 16 days later. NCMEC was created in 1984. When time is often the most important factor in finding a child alive, the organization acts as a force multiplier to protect children from abductors, online predators, and those who sexually exploit the young. They have their hands full supporting the investigations of missing minors, which could be as many as some 600,000 in the United States in any given year. Initially a fledgling organization, the group has grown to work with an annual budget of more than $45 million, funded primarily by federal tax dollars but staffed with dozens and dozens of volunteers, many of whom are retired law enforcement. But they focus only on children.

If this is going to work, they will need Lori Bruski on board. She is the regional coordinator who works as part of the team managing a federal database set up in 2007 to collect information, including DNA profiles, and help people directly enter and access information on the missing. The database is called the National Missing and Unidentified Persons System, or NamUs. The FBI's criminal forensic database is the Combined DNA Index System, or CODIS. Only law enforcement works in CODIS, but the public can work in NamUs.

The NamUs database is a secure, easy-to-use, and free online service anyone can use to search and share information about a missing person, including searching DNA profiles, information on missing people, and DNA found on a deceased but unidentified person. NamUs offers training on how to use the database, some free forensic services, and some free investigative support. NamUs is where Shannon plans to tap resources to get her DNA tested by the experts at UNT CHI. Since 2011, UNT CHI has handled the management of NamUs.

And, once the DNA profile is out there, it can be loaded into other private databases, such as Ancestry.com and other family DNA profile databases. Lori has been Shannon's contact at NamUs for years and knows the owners of these cemeteries from working on other cases. She'll be invaluable since she also has learned to interpret the cemetery maps, and it is handwritten notes on them that help to identify where a body might be buried. Numbers and letters are attached to everything, not just police files, but ME files, cemetery locations, body bags, and burial vaults. Everything seems to have a number, amplifying the impersonal nature of the situation.

When she first started handling missing persons cases, this is what struck Shannon the most. The sense of loss families must feel. It drove her to do more. A kid without a mom. A wife without a husband. A brother without a sister. Families would come to her office sometimes, but often Shannon was the only one looking at a file that had been abandoned as unsolvable. She was the only quasi-family left to mourn.

The cold case files represent a double punch to the gut for Shannon. Not only is a person missing, and the family is left without answers, but Shannon knows these are murder cases. Not only has a person been murdered, but a murderer has gone free.

Shannon begins to gather her team like beach glass, chatting with anyone she encounters in her daily activities. She needs helpful prosecutors, police from other departments, people who could learn the cemetery ways, forensic anthropologists, those who would dig, and investigators to follow leads. But she needed all the other things and people who could support a team working for several days. Maybe it won't be possible to identify all the 200 or 300 murdered people, but they must try.

She has so many questions. Could the killers still be alive? Are there family members even alive and do they care? What is a realistic goal? Investigators know murders are easier to solve when the victim's identity is known. That's a goal. But more important, she decides, is the missing person aspect of the case. She wants these unsolved, unknown victims, and cold case homicides to end up organized with a name on the top of each file. That is the first and most important goal.

Leslie agrees. Once identified, good investigative work could often win out. A person who went missing ten years ago may still have family who knew the victim's friends, their habits, their financial status, and work life. Identifying the victim inevitably results in scores of new leads. They can find loved ones to talk to about the murder victim. What does the family think happened?

From her many encounters with the family of the missing, Shannon recognizes that these families have a tape player looping in their brains. It plays what happened, what might have happened, what could have happened. Maybe they were confused or sick or simply wandered away. Maybe they left on their own and walked away. Maybe they were taken by someone who loved them, an estranged parent or someone who wanted access to their money. Maybe they encountered foul play, just another victim of random crime, in the wrong place at the wrong time. Maybe they were the criminal, running from the law. Maybe they were dead.

No matter, Shannon wants to get through each cold case homicide for the unknown; those records sitting stuffed into one of those boxes in the warehouse. She wants every lead followed on every case so she can say at least that these cases were solved or unsolvable. Those files haunting her from the warehouse had to be gone when she retired. She and Leslie check that off as the second goal.

CHAPTER 16

Solving Cold Case Homicides Is Hard

They agree their two additional goals, to find and then prosecute a murder, are possible but not so much in their control. The needed evidence isn't always attainable. There are a lot of ifs in Shannon's plan. If she could identify the potential murderer, and if she could find enough evidence for court, and if she could convince a prosecutor to file charges, and if there was a guilty verdict. Then, justice might be served. So many ifs. If evidence can be found, witnesses are willing to testify, and subjects are even available to be charged is asking a lot.

Even if all those factors come together, the people involved may not want a case resolved. A brother may have killed his brother, and no one is going to talk about it. A mother who abandons her unexpected child in an alley when she is 14 may be married with her own children and grandchildren now. They are long-buried secrets figuratively and literally.

Every year, plenty of murders go unavenged. Evidence disappears. It's not easier if a case is 30 or even 60 years old. Shannon won't let today's cases stop her from solving yesterday's murders. As plans come together, the business of today's investigations continues. She goes back to the warehouse for a new file when she has the time. But now her job is focused on leads above ground. The new plan leaves everything six feet under on Leslie's investigative to-do list.

"I would like to give people a definitive answer, like, 'No, your family was not recovered in Detroit,'" she says. "I can't say whether we have your loved one or not if I don't have all the DNA to compare it to. I need DNA from families."

When families do come to DPD headquarters, Shannon usually leaves them wanting more. Though they agree to contribute their own DNA for matching, she finds the results rarely match DNA on file. It's like an all-to-familiar blast of icy wind slapping her in the face as it comes off Lake St. Clair on a winter's day. With these older cases, people are more willing to give DNA samples because they are now more likely to accept the person may be dead.

"A lot of people that come forward are in their 30s," she explains the same day she takes DNA from a family whose mother has been missing since 1991. "Sometimes the call is from someone wanting to offer their DNA in hopes it will match the DNA of an unidentified dead person. But only a few new families show up each year. Sometimes people call saying they know about a missing person; sometimes it's an inmate calling to say they know something about a body or missing person.

"Around holidays I tend to get more requests, Mother's Day or Father's Day. A lot of times it's the children that come forward who have now grown up and are seeking answers because they have their own kids, and they don't know what to tell them. I never did think that I would be digging up dead bodies from a cemetery, but the real stress that I see is with families who are still missing somebody. It's one of the biggest motivations.

"I am doing my searches and I'm doing my intel work and looking through suspect profiles and different stuff like that. It's sad. The hardest to stomach are the women who have had a child disappear. I talk to these families and every month you know they text you or on a holiday, they get to me really good when they send me like a Happy Mother's Day, and I know that they're messed up and they're messed up 'cause it's Mother's Day and they don't have their child."

Detroit does solve cold cases occasionally, and Shannon is the one who notifies the families. It seems that would be a horrible task, but it is not.

"These families have been prepared for years," she says. "Ninety-five percent of them believe when I call them it's gonna be because we have them deceased. They already know that. They're already expecting that phone call, and they're hoping for that phone call."

The recently missing are different, she explains. "If somebody went missing today and I'm calling them tomorrow and telling them, 'We found your loved one deceased' that is gonna be a completely different shock factor because they're not prepared for it."

But where family members have waited months, years, or even decades, a call to come to the station brings together anguish and relief.

"On every single DNA notification I've ever had to give the number one reaction—they're hugging you, they're very happy, they take a big sigh— 'finally,'" she says. "And that's a terrible thought that you really are trying to process, but it's a thought that these families have been dealing with for years. These families are not shocked to hear it. This is what they've been waiting for."

They plan the first digs for 2019, a week in each of May, June, and July. Michigan outdoor life is great for hiking, skiing, and fishing. But digging in cemeteries is tricky when a yard of rain falls before the freeze and, on average, five feet of snow follows. That translates into fairly solid ground for maybe half of the year and soggy ground for most of the rest.

Leslie wants everything that can be found located in a single exhumation. No one wants to go back into a grave again. No one is by themselves down there. They are often two, three, or four deep. Some caskets or burial bags are in concrete vaults, some are not. Burial vaults might have two rows of bodies next to each other. If she pulls a casket at the top of a stack and then puts it back in, she better be sure she doesn't need the casket stacked two caskets down.

"We both kinda look at it from a practical standpoint, that is, we don't wanna crack a piece of ground repeatedly when we can crack it once," Leslie says, shifting to her all-business voice. "So that's what we're ...that's our long-term goal, really is to get all the files computerized into one central spot where we can take the files of the missing and unidentified folks, the burial records that we have from the cemeteries, even if they're off, and kind of zone those bodies, if you will, into different places within the cemetery. We deploy six, eight, ten dig teams right out in the field, we can't have an excavator on top of another excavator for safety reasons, but we wanna just make hot spots or compilations of bodies all over, so we can just kind of zone them."

It's a very sterile conversation to observers. They'll do the same thing the following years, Shannon adds. "We can knock the whole thing out in a few years before I retire. I figure I have about eight years to go." Shannon turns to Leslie. She cracks an ever so slightly detectable smile. "How much of the legwork is Leslie going to do?"

"Zero," Leslie replies with a bit of a chuckle in her voice. She looks for Shannon's reaction. They are developing a stilted but cohesive comradery.

"Shannon has that hard shell," Leslie says mostly to herself when Shannon turns away. "You can't let the goo out while you are working."

As she preps for the first dig, Shannon tells Leslie about the work she has already completed. She has located all the files for the first set of bodies and has isolated anything they can look for in a grave that tells them they have the right body. Sometimes it is clothes buried with the body. Other times it is little more than a height and potential sex. She has the court order from LaDonna that authorizes the searches of the cemetery graves. Leslie pulls her resources from far and wide.

But at the cemetery, everything is going wrong. It's May and the ground is a soggy mess. Plans call for digging in two cemeteries to look for the bodies, but they find one cemetery has pauper graves buried in such a poor location that the graves are essentially all but under water and unlocatable. Leslie's team can't dig where water is pouring in faster than they can drain every hole they start.

They move to the second cemetery, resolving to do better. They crack ground above the first grave. After an hour they realize what is underground doesn't match the cemetery records. Maybe it's a fluke.

They review the plans in the cemetery office. They try again. No luck. By week's end, they have only collected bones from one victim buried at Knollwood.

Trying to stay positive, they chalk May up to a learning lesson and move on to the plans for June. But June is an equal disaster despite their planning, all their knowledge, and all that sophisticated equipment. They pull away from United Memorial parking lot with only one set of bones they can submit for a DNA profile. The morass is both literal and figurative. And the people running the cemetery are very edgy about cooperating, remembering a situation in the not-too-distant past.

It seems, in 2018, United Memorial's cemetery services were severely curtailed after state licensing inspectors found more than 300 improperly stored infant and fetal remains in multiple crypts. In violation of standards and laws, the crypts had been opened and closed multiple times to add more bodies over a period dating back nine years. The accompanied news coverage was unwelcome and reminded Leslie that digging at any cemetery would require walking on eggshells.

Cemetery problems are more common than some imagine. For several years, a coalition of charitable organizations, including The Jewish Fund, committed $60,000 over several years to purchase "dignified" caskets to bury 200 other bodies stored in the Wayne County ME's office. Experts interviewed at the time blamed some of the backlog on the 2008 recession that left many families unable to afford a burial. Most were to be buried in Knollwood pauper graves, where unclaimed bodies were buried four deep in wooden boxes at unmarked grave sites. For a period, the cemetery was shut down temporarily by the owner based on a court order, stranding families who were trying to bury loved ones.

The new owners had made changes and promised improvements. They had even agreed to buy and place a grave marker for anyone they identified through Operation UNITED. Still, Shannon and Leslie had known showing up with a warrant to exhume dozens of bodies would make things tense.

Nothing seemed to have improved. They had dedicated a week in May and a week in June and had two bodies to show for it. Shannon's patience was waning. How many times can she tap these resources and ask restaurants and charitable organizations to send free food to support a week of digging when she tells them she has two of 200 bodies on her list? At this rate, it would take two decades to get the bones they needed.

With trepidation about the August dig, they head to United Memorial. They had learned from the earlier summer digs that the ground would likely be less sopped. They know better who to bring, what equipment to bring, and how to succeed in the digs. Still, the cemetery maps are baffling. They end the week with five successes. That bring the totals for the first year's digs to seven.

Back in the office, she knows she should be focusing on the next year's digs, but she's still stewing.

"You go out there with the mission to try to help something and you're trying to do something, and you got everything lined up and everybody is there and then you get that wrench thrown in there," she says, annoyed she even has to explain this. "You go through the emotions of 'This is someone's family and how could people back then treat people like that?'"

Angry but undeterred, Shannon and the team vow to shrug off the cemetery challenges, adjust, and do better the next year. She ships the bone fragments that were found and packed by the forensic anthropologists off to the UNT CHI for DNA analysis. Months pass, but Shannon's phone never rings with news that any DNA matches have been found.

With trepidation and winter days upon her, she begins prepping cases for the next season. The COVID-19 pandemic arrives. Coordination calls shift to video conference calls, texts, and email. While the rest of the country shuts down, police work does not. They need the momentum to continue. Shannon and Leslie return to more familiar solitary days in their offices.

Shannon's goal is to prep files and seek a court order to exhume another 25 bodies for the next dig season and find all of them along with those who they did not find the previous year. The women are not going to let that slow start be the standard. Shannon calls in favors, gathers volunteers, and borrows equipment and supplies for the next summer. Despite the disastrous results, she tells people to clear their calendars for the summer weeks and bring the items they need to succeed. They shift away from a May start, and dig in June, July, and August.

Everyone is relieved when they find 26 sets of bones the second year. These cases are the low hanging fruit. The cases where cemetery records were clean, and the case files were clear. A third year is ahead but still no word from the lab about a DNA match. Shannon heads to the warehouse. She needs a win.

Then, suddenly, her phone rings. Four, she says aloud. She dials Leslie.

"Four," she practically yells into the phone. UNT CHI researchers have extracted four profiles that match existing DNA. They have names of people whose names were forgotten. Their years of planning are bearing fruit. Operation UNITED is shining with its first successes.

Within days, Shannon is making her first identification call. She asks a man to come to the station. There is a boy, now a man, who lost his mom the night he went for a sleepover at his cousin's house. But now she is no longer lost.

They have given Anita Wiley back her name.

CHAPTER 17

Finding Anita

Roses in hand, Antonio Wiley arrives. The fog in his brain is from trying to process the call that led him to the Detroit cemetery. Both a glorious and torturous call has brought him here. The drive through rush hour traffic is no treat in an automobile town with no mass transit. He has taken the day off from his sometimes seven-day-a-week job. But this cemetery trip was required, and it is welcomed.

In a 10-minute conversation at police headquarters, Shannon told Antonio where he could find the mother he had not seen in 33 years. With the moxie required of a police officer, she also revealed one other horrifying detail.

Anita Wiley was brutally murdered.

"He sat down ... and we gave him that notification," she recalls, pausing again, choosing her words with precision. She leaves pause between each word. "He was ... very ... very ... happy about it."

She understands why he is happy. "There are a lot of emotions," she says. "This is X amount of years since he didn't know. Now this is the first year that he really knows the truth of where his mom was and he's processing all that stuff."

Antonio has no doubt chased through every possible terrifying and sad option in his idle moments. He finally has the most important answer; one that hopefully will lead to more truths and a murderer. He has a chance to write the final chapters of Anita Wiley's story. They are together again.

The murder investigation is to come, but first Shannon wants to give the family a bit of time. "It's a very emotional moment for families to be experiencing, and I don't want it to be anything about the case or the homicide or the circumstances," she explains. "Everything at that moment is about what they now know and where their sister, brother, father, [or] mother is."

Antonio heads west of his home. Easily mistaken for one of the surrounding fields of soybeans or corn, a functional green and white sign tells visitors they have instead found the cemetery on Curtis Avenue—paradoxically located off Joy Road. United Memorial Gardens is mostly flat; converted farmland perfectly suited for its task. From the road it might be mistaken for one of the surrounding fields used for rotating crops like soybeans or corn.

Shannon calls ahead. She needs someone at the cemetery to place a marker for Anita's grave. It's by a fence. It's family time and personal. Shannon doesn't want someone from the police department there.

"All you gotta do when you get up there, you're gonna go to this site, there's gonna be some tags," she tells him. "Read the tag." Somewhere in the sprawling 108 acres, Antonio is looking for a tree by a fence. Much of the cemetery is unfenced, drawing him toward the unkept gravel road closest to the nearby expressway.

He spies a stretch of the cemetery that abuts the interstate, a T-fence provides separation. It's the kind of fence used to keep cattle in or wildlife out. It's cheap and easy to put up when the prefab wire fencing is rolled out first. Just pound in a steel T-stake every 15 feet. Then, hook up the fencing that has eight horizontal rows of thin wire intertwined with vertical lines to create uniform six-inches squares.

A few pine trees stand close to Curtis Road and the interstate. That could be the spot, but it is not. Further down, a 40-foot Crimson King Norway maple tree glimmers in the sunlight and stands guard over a wide swath of ground. Its distinctive palm-sized red crimson leaves give away its pedigree.

The grass Antonio crosses is devoid of raised headstones. Close to the weather-beaten road, sporadic flat headstones identify mothers, fathers, sons, and daughters, most of whom had died around 1990. He would need to go the last 50 or so feet closer to the fence line. They'd told him to look for the tree by the fences. Only a few grave markers are visible, and many others are covered in leaves, pine needles, and untrimmed grass.

Speeding 18-wheelers amplify the already-noisy expressway din, disturbing the peace demanded. This is not the tranquil side of the cemetery. As he moves closer to the fence, the ground discloses more. He sees exposed dirt with scores of ants running across, and patches of dead grass remain, though it has been more than a year since digging had gone on there. Rocks, sticks, and anthills disrupt the way.

He can see a handful of red plastic flag tags zip-tied to the cattle fence near the pines and maple. The two-by-three-inch flags seem to be placed indiscriminately. Nearly all are blank, save one by the pine trees with the number 450 written in one-inch-tall numbers with a black permanent marker. The grave he was looking for needed a marker, but no one told him it was the impersonal marker number 450.

He needs her to not be a number. He needs her name to be there. She has a name. Thirty-three years is long enough. It is hard for him to believe that Anita Wiley is not just a nameless person buried in a bag among the hundreds of paupers' graves at United Memorial.

He had been only 14 when it happened. Truthfully, he could not really say what had happened. He just knew his mother was not there when he moved on from that relentlessly uncomfortable age of 14 into his high school years. She was not there when the apartment phone got disconnected. She was not there when he had to leave their apartment. She was not there when he shaved for the first time or went on his first date. She was not there when he got his first job, bought his first car, found his first home, or held his first child.

When Antonio spoke to police he didn't really know much about if, or when, the police were called. He was only told they were. He didn't know if they had a file. He was a teen trying to navigate classes and learn about girls. He didn't remember very much. He knew it was 1987. He lived with his mother. She had given him permission to stay overnight at a cousin's house.

"She kissed me, told me she loved me, and would see me the next day," he later told a local news reporter. Then Anita Wiley left to go to the store and slipped into the darkness forever.

Antonio returned the next day, but Anita did not.

"Every day you know, I just kind of hoped that would be the day that she would come home," he recalls. "Days turned into weeks, months to years."

Uncertain if police were doing anything to find his missing mom, Antonio carried on, living with relatives, and got on with his life. He kept the information to himself as best he can. Minors can't live on their own.

But Anita Wiley did not carry on. Pieces of her were found months later, not far from their apartment. She had no identification, and the ME verified the cause of death as murder, strangulation. Another manilla-tabbed file stuffed with what was known about unknown Black woman #1987.

"A lot of people had a lot of opinions about what they thought happened, but it really didn't give me answers," Antonio says. "So, one day I just decided to start over." He visited a local fair and stopped at a table with a sign that said "Missing in Michigan." He doesn't know he is the only one who stops by that day. He meets a person from DPD.

"I don't know if there is a file," Shannon tells him, but she assures him she will open a new one. She types the information he provides into her laptop and takes a cheek swab. Impossible to know at the time, she had just recently push-pinned Anita Wiley's information onto her *Who Am I?* wall. It is four years before Operation United begins.

Anita was the first identified, but three others followed from that first dig. Their files were more complex and, as with many cases, disclosing things prematurely risks interfering with potential murder charges. Family members might be involved, and it take time to sort things out. But for now, they had the most important piece needed—a name.

"When she says she's got one, it makes your day," Leslie says. "It makes that time away from your family worth it. To be able to give those remains back to that family member. It's so important to show the family that we in law enforcement haven't given up." Family is so important to Leslie.

Her close but small family has always been everything to Leslie. She had asked to be assigned to the FBI's Detroit office so she could drive home to the family farm whenever she wanted to see her folks. In the house they helped her buy, her father laid flooring and built a deck. She had dated some, yet work always pushed aside personal time. But then she met Virginia Ann. Virg, as Leslie calls her, is also in law enforcement. They get the pressures of each other's jobs. They know about nights when you can't come home and don't have time to call to explain why.

They marry in October, the fall before the first dig. It is a beautiful day in Michigan. A friend's country home provides the perfect setting as guests sit on bales of hay and the couple exchanges vows, each dressed in a long white formal. The memories are captured forever as the sun begins to set in the sky. They pose for photos by the wagon and then the fence and then the corn stalks.

For Leslie, it is an instant family, her with her unruly hair she kept nearly blond and Virg with her dark hair. She seems to need family, and she settles quickly into the new role of second mom to Virg's two kids. Together they split kid duties, decorating their new home together and hovering over the kitchen table to make sure homework is completed. At night, they often slip out to their small back deck to watch the sunset and find a wine cooler from the stock.

When they identify Anita Wiley, she feels the impact of re-connecting families and finding murdered children. Her new reality re-energizes her in an intimate and unanticipated way for the next season's dig, still one winter away. It will be easier. After a couple of dig seasons, everyone in her business wants to work the Operation UNITED digs.

Leslie can draw her team from the cream of the crop of those who are trained to collect evidence or dig. Together they have discovered hundreds of bodies. They collected evidence for drug, bank robbery, and major white-collar prosecutions. Her team worked terrorist cases tough to get into court.

Before the next dig, Leslie and Shannon sit down to plot how to best dig in common areas and spread their teams out. No one needs two excavators crossing paths, as they learned the hard way. They know Lori is at the cemetery office, comparing cemetery records to what she can find in the NamUs files.

Shannon and Leslie schedule pre-dig week visits to mark all the graves with the guidance of cemetery managers. A wooden stake with a flat triangle of plastic with a note tied to it ensures they will scrape soil as close as possible to their targets buried underground. It would be easier. They'd learned so much from the experience of the first two years. No more digging in soggy May. Leslie's philosophy is to evolve and try to do better. Stay positive.

"We had a couple of negative wrenches that were thrown in there, but we are all very motivated," she said. "No one was saying, 'I'm giving up, lets cancel this project, it's a bad idea.' Instead, it's 'Alright, realize we need to go out there ahead of time, take photos, locate GPS spots of cases that we got confirmed so when we have somebody identified and we GPS that specific location, it will help us to locate the other cause we're going off of that GPS spot.'"

Each dig season, Shannon and Leslie go to the cemetery the night before to mark the graves as best they can. Shannon has coordinated above ground, tracking down volunteers and working with cemetery management as dig dates approach.

They choose dig dates when the cemetery can be closed to visitors completely or the paupers graves can be blocked off from visitors. No one wants to come to a cemetery and see open vaults and blue tarps covered with remains. It's a lesson learned. During the first dig, Shannon had to stop a family headed to a grave with flowers. They were disappointed, but surprised when Shannon herself offered to walk the flowers to the grave. She understood.

When they go out to do reconnaissance on the next dig, they head to where the paupers graves lie along the cheap fence between the expressway and the 108-acres cemetery. Shannon approaches the King Norway where a fence tag still marks Anita Wiley's grave. A bouquet of flowers lays atop dead leaves and sticks.

Antonio has found his mom.

CHAPTER 18

Shredded Files and Budget Cuts

Energized with the success of their news about Anita Wiley, all seems to be going according to schedule. Until it is not.

Without fanfare, Shannon is notified that Wayne County is going to shred all the police files in the county's warehouse. Officials have decided to abandon the paper file system that housed the historical DPD files, and all the old case files will be shredded as a cost-saving measure. Nothing will be digitized, so the information in the files will be lost forever.

Files for missing persons and cold case homicides are mixed in with files for bank robberies, car thefts, and domestic abuse calls. Everything is mixed in big banker's boxes. She can't just carry all the boxes away. She'd like to have every cold case homicide victim file in her control, but she's not sure how many there are, or how to find them. Still, she'll figure out a way.

She has a week or so to get it done.

If they want to pull any files, they can come the next Wednesday, she is told. That is when the only person with the only key will be there to let them in. It is such a government problem and such a government answer to say only one person has the key.

Undaunted, she calls Leslie.

"I can develop a list of files to fish for if you can bring hands," Shannon says. Maybe a lot of hands?

Keen to the finality of the situation, she also begins trying to identify "unidentified" cases from other police agencies located in Wayne

County, not just Detroit police files. Other police jurisdictions won't even know their files are on the way to the shredder.

She has a plan. Shannon and Leslie both love a good plan. It keeps them focused and takes a bit of emotion away from the execution. Emotion makes police work messy. She'll meet Leslie the next day.

When Shannon arrives, however, she sees Wayne County personnel pulling boxes off the shelves. What the hell. She has once chance to get 60 or so years of files and this is happening.

She starts to pull files. Leslie meets up with her, but as they try to pull files, the boxes are disappearing. Maybe this isn't worth it. It would be so much easier just to let them go. No one has asked about those files for decades. She could look the other way and say she did her best to battle county frustrations. No one would question that.

But she and Leslie would know. They would always know that they could have done more. Tried harder. Cared more. Calm, she thinks, just another obstacle.

Leslie is there and "tones out" her entire 40-member team, asking for anyone who is available to come and help. Within the hour, six members of the team roll in to work the day. After a few calls, three more from Shannon's office arrive.

The day becomes a kind of game of hide and seek. Shannon is telling everyone who shows up what to look for on the file jackets, the shorthand that indicates missing or murdered and unidentified.

While Wayne County employees look for boxes to stack on their carts and take to the shredder. Leslie, Shannon, and other team members move strategically through aisleways, subtly interfering with their ability to move the carts around. Shannon is pulling files as fast as she can find them, and they are talking to each other under and over the metal shelves to confirm whether to pull a file and what box to preserve it in so it won't be shredded. Now nearly a dozen people are trying to match Shannon's suspected files with something in a box. The team is sifting through as many files as possible just to be sure, as others stand between the boxes and the Wayne County carts.

Their message of defiance becomes clear, and an hour or so in, the workers relent somewhat and wait, if a little impatiently, for files to be pulled and the box handed over to the death cart.

Despite the perturbing start, the day is pretty much a success. Shannon estimates 95 percent of the files she wants are in her car. It might not be all the files, and they'll never know for sure. Are they leaving cold case murders forever unsolved because of the file destruction? Are the people who cry budget constraints simply people who don't care about those cold case murders?

"Pulled all the unidentified we could," Leslie texts to a friend. "Rest of files are getting shredded. So sad." These are the only records of any autopsy files, unless some of the copies made it into a DPD investigative file; otherwise, they are lost forever. And, Leslie says, "You never want to rely on that." Pedantic government rules are her bane.

Now all the remaining available files are in Shannon's overcrowded space, but at least they have been saved. When COVID-19 displaced everyone in the office in some way or another, Shannon had taken the opportunity to expand her territory to other "pods" and any available file cabinet or flat surface. Notwithstanding the warehouse scare, the digs themselves are becoming like well-oiled machines with less surprises and more predictability. Three each summer for the first two summers. For the upcoming third season, she wants to prep 60 or more cases and pulls out her spreadsheets to assess the status of Operation UNITED.

Shannon begins her work on files, hoping as the winter snow flies that she will be able to meet with the women for a day of information sharing where they go through all the files they have, develop a to-do list, and prioritize the next summer's dig schedule. She asks what day works for Leslie, Lori and their teams to get together to go through spreadsheets and the files nearly lost in the train crash at the warehouse?

She already has several dozen sets of bone samples at UNT CHI in Fort Worth, Texas, for DNA testing. Why aren't they getting back results, she asks Lori, frustrated at the pace. "It's just going to take time," Lori reassures her. But weeks before they are scheduled to review cases, she hears more frustratingly bad news.

The UNT CHI partnership with the government is crumbling. It's true, the university announces in December, that its ten-year management of NamUs is ending "due to funding limitations and significant program modifications directed by the National Institute of Justice [NIJ]." Shannon has lost her source for DNA testing. It looks like Lori is out of a job, too.

Shannon asks around. Who else knows DNA who could do the testing. To find a DNA profile, a small bone sample is cut, and a demineralizing solution is applied first. It takes time, but the amount of DNA needed to produce a visible profile is small. In fact, they only need to find about one nanogram of DNA to be able to take an image of the bar-code looking markers for comparisons with other markers. A nanogram is one billionth of a gram or about one thirtieth of an ounce. That's the same size as a human cell. Not just any lab can do it.

"DNA analyses are complicated," Jodi says. "It's not like NCIS."

After they acquire a sample, the true work begins as they look for identifying markers. Special reagents are used to extract and purify the DNA from that bone. Only then, if a profile is successfully obtained, can it be uploaded into CODIS and other appropriate databases.

If a bone came into her university lab today, Jodi guesses, she and her coworker could have the DNA testing done in about four days, but only if they just dropped everything and did nothing else.

Jodi can't help Shannon by running the tests in her college labs and neither can the offices where other scientists supporting Operation UNITED work, including Jane, the Director at the FROST Center, or the five women running the Body Farm: Giovanna Vidoli, Joanne Devlin, Dawnie Steadman, Lee Meadows Jantz, and Mary Davis. Their mission's focus must remain on research and training.

She calls Leslie and asks if the FBI can run all the DNA. Some, Leslie says, but not likely all. There are limits on the number of samples the FBI can take, and they have their own priorities to manage. She's not sure the FBI Laboratory at Quantico would be willing to take on all of the Operation UNITED murder cases. She's not sure they'll take any. Maybe next year's digs will need to be canceled.

Weeks go by. The usual bleakness of Detroit's cloud-covered winter sky seems even darker. Shannon receives word not to send any more bones for testing. Maybe this is it for Operation UNITED. Maybe her dream of closing 200 plus cold cases murder will end at four.

Because she finds the time at work, Shannon continues to rummage through files, looking for new leads and isolating the cases that have nowhere to go without DNA.

Leslie, too, hasn't given up. She files her funding request with FBI Headquarters, hoping to get money for the next summer's dig. She can't pay for all the additional gloves and bags and tarps and water pumps with her current funds, let alone pay to bring FBI personnel from other offices. She stands on the sidelines and waits.

More weeks go by. Then Lori calls. If the threat to stop testing was a ploy to get more money by UNT CHI, she explains, it has worked. At least it has worked for now. A week later, NIJ officials announce publicly that UNT CHI has accepted a new $4.3 million grant. But the bear has been poked. Two days later, NIJ puts out a "request for proposal," a mechanism that will allow any eligible company to bid to manage NamUs in the future. All they can do now is wait and hope that another testing lab will be chosen.

Taking no chances, they agree that going forward. Two bone samples will be pulled from each body found. Leslie will keep one in her evidence vault at FBI Detroit. If they can't get DNA samples in a new testing lab, Leslie assures Shannon she'll try to get them processed through the FBI lab in Quantico, Virginia. She keeps to herself that she doesn't know if this can be done.

As if to tease, one more DNA profile trickles in. That's five, Shannon thinks. Not the splash she anticipated when she sold this idea to Leslie. After three years of work, destroyed files, and no sure place to test bones, their detailed and contingency-filled plan seems more as if they are trying to catch smoke between their fingers.

Anxious to get off the ledge she's stuck on, Shannon revises her way forward. She'll filter through all the outstanding files, including the warehouse files at one time. Shannon calls the other women leading the effort to see if they are all in. They agree that bringing all the disparate information together should provide their best chance at a comprehensive wish list of buried treasures.

She will need to match her information with Lori's databases and all of Leslie's notes from the six digs during the past two years. She discusses the plan with Leslie, whose teams have unearthed and moved plenty of people, boxes, vaults, and bags. Details of every movement is documented, including noted GPS coordinates. Even the vaults and bodies found by mistake can help in the mapping of future digs.

"Once we got Anita," Leslie explains in an upbeat tone, "we can measure from Anita if somebody was buried before her or after, and we know that it is gonna be X amount of feet this way or that way. So now with more DNA hits, we should be able to–it should make things easier."

That's essential not only for finding victims, but also for returning bones after testing. Once DNA has been extracted, they put the bones back. It requires double the digs, but Leslie and Shannon are determined their actions won't add to the indignities already suffered by these victims.

Digging can be more strategic this way. Once Shannon evaluates all the files, she can decide how many more digs they still might need. Forewarning, Leslie advises that the FBI has still not released any funding for the first dig in July. She can't call an audible on funding. She has no backup plan.

February, March, and April pass, but still, she has no funding for the project that will give her the needed equipment, people, flights, hotel rooms, and food to bring in her specialist dig teams from other FBI field offices. The $25,000 she obtained for the first dig seems so far away now.

Her own management in Detroit is dismissive. An impatient executive demands to know, "How hard can it be to find a dead guy in a cemetery?" As he drones on, she thinks to herself, "It's not like I have a fish finder and we're in a fishing boat."

She checks and discovers her funding request is stuck somewhere in FBI Headquarters. She begins texting and calling people. No one is answering. She asks for advice from other agents and retired friends, and places call after call to find a time when, hopefully, she can catch the attention of a busy headquarters executive who is interested in the digs. She just needs one inspired executive. She beats the bushes.

Her best FBI sources for navigating bureaucracy are suggesting she tag team all her potential funding sources: the Laboratory, the Criminal Investigative Division, and her own field division, Detroit. She's hearing the Lab is short on funds because some other program is out of cash. What does that mean? She thinks. Frustrated, she asks aloud, doesn't anyone know how important this program is and how it shows that the FBI is helping to show law enforcement never gives up and will be there when the local departments are limited?

Her text exchanges read with a mixture of futility and hope; "I'm not giving up," "Still fighting. We are all leaving messages. No answers back." "Other calls have failed." "We won't have a program if we don't have funding." "It will go no matter what, it just may look different, like maybe two weeks instead of three. Way fewer bodies recovered."

Determined, Shannon and Leslie text back and forth to nail down a date to sort all the files into one final comprehensive list. Lori joins in. She seems two steps ahead of everyone and it is evident she is brilliant and a vital part of their overall effort. Leslie can bring two from her team and have them put all the available information onto Excel spreadsheets to project on the wall. They can print them into huge sheets to hang. They'll do the file sorting knowing there is no funding and with only a handful of bones identified. Is it worth it three years into the effort?

The two confer. They have been able to overcome any problem they have encountered, they agree. Their tenacity won't let them stop midway. It's not in their nature.

With no FBI funding secured, they schedule a May meeting at police headquarters to review the details of every *Who Am I?* and *Where Am I?* file that exists. On the eve of the meeting to prep files, North Carolina-based RTI International, an independent, nonprofit research institute, announces it has been awarded the bid and will take over the management of NamUs and the related DNA testing labs. Posturing and airing of dirty laundry by UNT CHI has lost them the contract and put more gray hairs on Shannon's and Leslie's heads. At least now they have someplace to send the bones.

They think about how Antonio's life has changed. They are more determined than ever to clear the books on every cold case homicide.

CHAPTER 19

Another Dead Baby

1955. File Number 1.

A 7-month-old, premature baby has been discovered by a neighbor, frozen in an alley off Blaine Street, a cord wrapped around the baby's neck.

The day begins painfully. A harrowing start.

They will sift through the information they have on homicide cases to see if there is enough for a match to the contents of a coffin that might be in a vault where three or more coffins are stacked on top of each other. Or maybe to a spot where the body was buried, not even in a box, in a cemetery on the edge of the county.

The goal for the day is to identify potential files with enough hints inside that they have enough confidence that digging for a body might allow them to extract missing DNA. If they secure this cornerstone of a cold case homicide, they will have something to go on. Then digging, testing, and investigating might prod a prosecutor in the Wayne County district attorney's office to consider charges, the first step toward a murder conviction.

Those would be the home runs. They know a baseball fan would see many of their successes as hits with runners stranded at the end of the inning. That's OK. Every baseball player steps up secretly hoping for that home run.

The windows on a far wall light the training room. Furnishing is sparse save for long worktables and hard plastic chairs. Carpet that is dark enough to hide foot traffic compels the silence required in a suburban library. They are off a corridor at Shannon's headquarters, just blocks from Lake St. Clair where the Detroit River carries water between Lake Huron and Lake Erie.

Cardboard boxes have been lugged in. A glow from the dim projector lamp points toward the wall where the windows are, but the room remains dark enough that entering it requires a movie-theater adjustment for the eyes.

A bit of sunlight allows them to leave the overhead lights off in the training room as Leslie's team projects an Excel spreadsheet up on a screen. The spreadsheet is designed to pull all the information together, whether from a paper file, electronic police files, or information found in records they have from NamUs, cemeteries, or the ME's office. Leslie's assistant has taken weeks to pre-load details from 110 files rescued from destruction at the Wayne County warehouse.

Several tables away, Lori has spread her belongings across a large training table of her own. Her laptop lets her review cemetery records and search NamUs at will. In her corner, she will review these records to verify the possible burial locations of unknown children and adults. They are in the system and tagged with vague and impersonal names like "unknown female baby #3" or "unknown male #31."

But File Number 1 yields no hope for an easy day.

"No details in NamUs" Lori yells from across the room. No one seems to have reported a missing baby around that location in 1955. No one knows the NamUs system inside and out like Lori. Her mind is a vault of a different kind.

Shannon looks to her cemetery records to verify. She can't find a female baby buried in United Memorial in 1955. They've already hit a hard stop.

They move on.

"The 1956 cases are two fetuses and a skull found by a man," one of Leslie's crew calls out. There are scant details. They recognize that earlier cases are tough because there will be few details.

That 1957 skull case? The investigative file shows that it has a neat hole drilled in it and it appears to be an anatomical specimen. It comes off the list.

"We should get those black books that show when the body came into the ME's office," Lori suggests aloud to no one in particular. But maybe she is directing.

Leslie understands. She leans over and adds "get medical examiner logs" to her to-do list, saying aloud, "I'll get those in and scanned."

Lori has spent many hours in the offices with cemetery staff, poring over records to better understand the business. It's a love-hate relationship with the cemeteries. Lori has perfected navigating those waters, so when she says the MEs records are needed, they all know she'll be proven right. The bodies are there, but the record keeping hasn't been the best over the years.

Every so often, a cemetery changes ownership and all the hand notation on maps and files needs to be interpreted by the new owner and team. At one point, someone decided to write some burial information on a piece of wood, Lori discovered. So that is part of the official records. Burial boxes shift underground, reacting to water and nearby construction.

At the cemeteries, they work outside, but to prep for a dig day, they work inside. No amount of funding for personnel or having all the right equipment matters if they don't know who to dig for and where to dig. Cemetery records might indicate ten people collected from the ME's office and buried at the same time to save the county costs. For the unnamed who might be buried, it all starts with those paper files.

Shannon is thankful the women have found a day to meet for this essential but grim task. It helps to temper emotions. Leslie's team, Becca and Kelsey, are manning the electronic Excel spreadsheet and the backup resource, a paper copy printed on four sheets of three-foot by four-foot-wide printer paper. They are taped to the wall.

"Paper backup is good," Leslie says, encouragingly. Beside her is the file box with the original documents.

Leslie is keeping track of her to-do list. By day's end, it will include notes to reach out to several police departments on files determined to have been initiated outside Detroit, but in another department's jurisdiction and needing more investigative work.

Shannon must track down missing information from the Detroit files. Those are cases that can't go on a dig list without more work. Shannon's other box of battered manilla files—about 75—are already prepped for a dig. Another 30 were prepped for digging last year, but for a host of reasons that didn't happen.

The day's tasks include determining what unknowns in a cemetery may match a file and then evaluating the likelihood of digging that body up, including how to get around other caskets. Shannon has been prepping nearly 100 additional files that need to be considered. With others added through the day, the pair will be able to develop specific plans for future digs. It's a lot of dead people.

While Leslie scans through the new information for each case on the Excel sheet, Shannon sits behind her, tapping into Detroit police databases.

"Damn it," Shannon exclaims loudly, but mostly to herself, "another dead baby. These are the ones that I want to find the most. And then I want to find the mother and …" Sometimes she finishes the sentences. Sometimes she doesn't.

They read a file about a buried one-week-old girl who had frozen to death in 1990 and was malnourished when she died.

"Knollwood," Lori reports.

"Great," Leslie and Shannon say together, knowing it is easier to dig there.

"Prayer Extension," Lori adds a moment later, identifying the section in the cemetery where they will have to dig.

Optimism turns to multiple gasps of exasperation. Leslie and Shannon look at each other.

Prayer Extension is wet and deep; eight feet deep. It's hard to have a successful dig. They mark it for a dig nonetheless and move on.

Shannon has also brought a file box with all the open cases on her *Who Am I?* and *Where Am I?* walls that are still missing DNA profiles. "The files match wall photos, each with a yellow sticky tab on them," she explains. It makes it easier to be sure she has them all.

Belongings and files carried in are now spread out all over each person's own table to allow everyone to dig for information that will fill in the Excel spreadsheet columns. Lori knows her files well and is offering up possible cemetery locations and NamUs numbers and information.

The big color-coded spreadsheets are being updated by hand to show progress.

Some of the 36 cases already targeted for the upcoming dig season are listed. The master sheets keep things in order. Blue highlight lines mean the cases were prepped for a dig last season, but the bodies weren't located. There are 27 of those. Three white entries identify prepped cases the dig teams couldn't get to, and they were returned to the cardboard boxes under Shannon's desk to sit through the long, icy Michigan winter. Those are the first priorities for dig season: what they could not find the year before.

The 29 yellow and orange entries signify cases where bones have been located and Operation UNITED is well underway. They have bones either at a laboratory or waiting to be sent to a lab for DNA analysis. The labs, even the vaunted FBI Laboratory, will only take a few new samples a month to ensure cold cases and new cases are both addressed.

A handful of lines stand out. Those are the entries where a successful dig has had a successful DNA analysis from their first dig season. "Getting to this step is a tremendous and unnecessarily long process," Leslie explains. On this depressing day, they have six matches, six names, and they are still in the early stages with the DA's office. Some families are beginning to be notified, and the DA's office is trying to turn names into prosecutable cases.

What about the solo red line? "Dug by mistake," Leslie admits. Cemetery digs are tricky. Bones are everywhere.

Today, however, they are focused on one line at a time. Leslie's team helps read and type from the narrow rows on the paper Excel sheets they all see projected on the wall. The spreadsheet is raw information filled with hundreds of entries on dozens of columns—a simple but effective method of bringing all the information to one spot. The sheet identifies those cases with enough information and a potential cemetery location to be able to dig. By putting everything together, Leslie, Shannon and Lori can plot out who to dig up, and in what order. Calculate twice, dig once.

Shannon assures that Detroit has a case file number for each cold case homicide. The ME's office also has file numbers, as does the FBI. Then there might be file numbers belonging to the Michigan State Police or another involved police department. NamUs has numbers. Prosecutor offices have numbers. Missing person databases have numbers. Other offices may have opened a case or sent investigators with information. A buried body has a numbered cemetery vault connected to it, or what might be the cemetery vault.

Basics fill the columns. Where was the body found? Was the body clothed? Are there pictures of the bullet wounds, the teeth, the smashed skull? What tests did the ME run? MEs might have dental imprints or photos of items found with a body or body parts. If a missing person case began in a neighboring town, its file number might lead to other investigative efforts.

The details between the lines are sobering. "Man and wife found the body floating in the river." "Newborn baby found laying (sic) nude on a trunk in a basement." "Body found floating in the river."

Nearby these sobering entries: "found burned in a trash receptacle in rear of Cass Tech High School." "Left leg was separated with foot still intact, but the tibia and fibula have been charred and burned." "Decomposing baby found in a garbage can." "Baby found in a box." "Fetus was found partially burned in a trash can." "Baby found in alley." "Body parts found at the base of a 25-foot sewer blocking the sewer pipe."

Concentration is key. Eyes are strained. Judicious use of words helps as everyone who is poring over their own disparate notes and shouting out additional details. No one can afford mistakes.

As the morning progresses, they struggle to find victories, but they find some. Because they are going through files in chronological order, a case opened after a murder victim is found may mean that the resulting ME's file and burial records might also be in that time period.

The converted casino that is police headquarters has a disproportionately large kitchen and could accommodate food for a wedding reception. No vending machines here. But the pandemic has conspired to limit any cooking on site. A food truck has brought in barbequed ribs and wings for the police and fire personnel in the building. Leslie can't eat ribs.

Lori remains wired into the NamUs site and is off working in a corner of the training room, mining information from the system. Some of the cases have been updated to add a name where someone outside the group has validated an identity. Those cases will be removed from the list of potential dig subjects.

They review two homicide cases back-to-back—a decomposed body of a man at the train station and another man found murdered and left for dead in a vacant dwelling. It turns out they were buried together, one after the other. Then, they find a third unidentified murder victim, a man found in the Detroit River and buried at the same time.

Translation: the team will be able to dig once but potentially find three bodies.

"I like the three for one," Lori says, revealing her undertaker's grin.

"That's amazing," adds Leslie. "We should give that to a new team leader, so they get three wins. We should give the Indiana [FBI] team that one."

Often the conversation begins with bones in a bag or wrapped in tissue. They scroll down the master sheet but there is no more information, which means it is moved over to Shannon's list to try to resolve. Baby deaths usually have few details to provide. White, Colored, or Negro is listed, depending on the age of the file. Most babies were found naked, but wrapped in something nondescript. There are few clues to rely on. No teeth imprint or photographs. No scars. No hair. A baby's eye color changes and darkens when exposed to light, so even eye color may not be useful. The older cases are challenging.

When they break for lunch, there are only three orange highlighted cases.

"At least we have some on the board," Leslie says.

"And we're getting a lot off of the list," Lori adds.

They discover four other cases are tied together and remove them from Leslie's sheets. One had a first name of Keith. In 2007, Keith's body was cut into pieces. Investigation resulted in the four different cases now being tied together. Keith's head was found in a bag on a porch. His jawbone was found elsewhere. His bullet-ridden and stabbed body, or parts of it, was found buried at two other locations. In 2013, DNA from body parts identified him through offender DNA, resolving the identity question, if not the murder.

"Offender DNA" means the DNA match was found in a law enforcement database on criminal offenders. Who does that to a person and cuts them into four pieces? They'll try to find out, but not right now. Operation UNITED is focused first on identification. Investigations must come later.

When they walk the hallway past the carpeted waiting areas to the cafeteria, visitors surely are unaware of the nature of work that is taking place beyond the entrance.

CHAPTER 20

Babies, Bodies, and Bones

They are on a new year: 1958.

Unknown skeleton number 1.

They are mentally transported back to March 27, 1958. The case involves two boys digging in the dirt near a house in the suburb of Livonia. Back then, Livonia was more farmland and pastures than shopping centers and movie multiplexes. More like Leslie's childhood farm than the Livonia she lives in today.

The two boys found a few bones, and then more. They are human. Police discover a small girl's ring on the skeleton. The body appears to be that of a teenage girl, buried nude. But as they look at more markers, the reports suddenly turn to details that seem to also describe a 30-year-old male. They can't find a "cemetery ticket" that might indicate where the body was buried.

The records aren't clear enough to put it on the cemetery list. Lots of details, but not the right ones. Leslie volunteers to stop by the Livonia police to see if they have any more information and if they want to join back in to help solve the case. It's one more item on the to-do list.

The next file is also dated March 27, 1958, but it involves unknown bones found near the city of Hamtramck, a suburb surrounded by the city of Detroit. Police received an anonymous call stating that a child had been "burned up" at 9816 Hindle St. Arriving police officers are compelled to break into the house to gain entry. They don't find anybody inside, but they do come upon ash and bones in an ash burner. The ME's notes further illuminate that the remains appear to be those of a 28-week-old baby delivered early, when the mother was about seven months along. The ME concludes that infant #2452 was burned to death by the mother who had delivered it herself, secretly, then looked to discard it. It's not enough to go on for a dig now, but maybe with more investigative work, Shannon can make progress on the murder investigation that flailed 60 years earlier. Shannon, too, ironically, is focused more on the low hanging fruit.

Someone calls out the date of April 24, 1958.

"That case needs to be closed," Shannon instructs.

This is file number #2452 with a skull discovered by a man digging in his backyard. Police department notes say this is only the jawbone from the skull of a female. It's not enough information. Leslie adds the file number to her list. She'll stop by the Melvindale police station to see if they have any more in their closed file.

"Number 2739 is another baby," Lori says aloud. Though everyone in the room has no doubt already made the connection, she adds, "abortion was taboo in the 50s."

Leslie voices the details without emotion: body found wrapped in a towel, put in a bag, left in the middle of the street. Homicide notified. Nationality/race is listed as colored, April 26, 1958. The deceased is listed as having been alive at birth and dead when found about two days later. The ME confirms it is a homicide.

Lori is looking at the records for the cemeteries. "There is an unknown girl #3 who was buried in 1958 in Babyland," Lori shares.

"They buried them in bulk," Shannon explains flatly. "They held them and submitted them all at once."

They agree to leave it as a possible United Memorial match for a burial plot tagged as Babyland #2, grave site #148. If no other unknown #3 female babies show up, this might be a match. If they can get a potential cemetery location, it can be marked in orange on the big flowcharts. It's one of the first new ones for the dig list. They move on.

Homicide victim, unknown man #34, is from May 1958. He was wearing long underwear and a three-piece suit, a well-nourished White male, five feet seven, 170 pounds. Lori volunteers the ME's conclusion: suffocation by drowning. He was found floating in the water by the Southfield dock, just south of River Rouge, a town a few miles north of Detroit.

"It's not many details," Leslie says, and adds another file number to her to-do list to remind herself to stop at a local police department. Maybe they will have more details or be willing to work on the cold case.

Next, from the city of Inkster, is unknown baby girl #6. Another police department for Leslie to stop by. What they know is that a baby girl was found wrapped in a blanket in a field. The next 1958 file, case number 3401, is from May 29, 1958, and involves bones found during a freeway excavation near Connors and Gunston streets. It's listed as a Detroit homicide.

"Unidentified homicide victims are buried in an area of the cemetery that is a swampland a good portion of the year," Shannon says, speaking what they all know about the challenges. "Others are buried along the freeway."

"That's a perfect reason to do this in September," Leslie says, no doubt thinking of her team's ability to fish bones from water-laden and crumbling boxes.

Since Shannon's hope is to permanently resolve the cold case homicides, she has gathered every case she can find that meets these criteria, including cases that perhaps were miscategorized. They move on. Unknown floater #38 is a man found drowned, approximately 50 years old. Shannon needs to do more research before they can decide if they have enough information.

Finally, they reach the year 1959. First on the list is a baby, #5, a man found in a cardboard box on Bayside Street. The 16-inch-long premature baby was wrapped in newspaper and listed as unknown "fetus." Lori identifies two potential burial sites, but the information is so scant they can't be sure the burials are matching. "Baby #5 needs more research," Leslie declares. With a plan to resolve issues on that case before the dig dates arrive, it goes on Shannon's to-do list.

The afternoon slogs on. The gray sky outside is as still as the stuffy air inside. The files involving adults are easier to match to a potential burial site because each coffin or bag has one body in it, which also might include clothes and personal items that were buried with the body. Adult files have more details, such as death date, nature of injuries, height, and other markers.

Unknown fetus #9, "apparently colored," is file #2276. The full-term male infant had second and third-degree burns and a fracture on one arm. The file notes indicate the body was "colored," but was burned after birth to obscure identifying factors. Leslie will have to stop by the local police department to see if more details exist.

Shannon moves on to file #6121, a male fetus, a likely stillborn four-pound baby that was found on October 9, 1959 in an incinerator at 2701 Hastings St.

"Are we still on babies?" Leslie complains.

"There's a playground there on Hastings," Kelsey pipes up.

"There are a lot of incinerator babies; it's fucking horrible," mumbles Shannon to no one as she shakes her head and pulls out another file from her box.

"More research for you, Shannon," Leslie directs.

"A lot of Shannon work going on here," Shannon says sternly to the crowd.

"Just four so far," Kelsey says.

"I've got my own list," Leslie says. "I have five."

They move on to the last of the 1950s cases. It's another unknown fetus, #30, discarded in Rouge Park, a neighborhood west of downtown Detroit.

That totals 30 unknown dead babies found in Wayne County that year.

"It may have taken a breath or two," Kelsey says, noting the ME's report on a baby found deceased. "That's so sad."

The first case of the 1960s is just a child's finger. They can't work with that, Shannon says. That file comes off the list.

"The 60s are starting off well," Leslie says sarcastically.

Shannon flips open the next file folder. Burned body of a male baby lying on top of the ashes in a trash can, a full term, colored male. This is now another contender for unknown baby #3.

"That could be the United Memorial Babyland #2, 148 location," Leslie says, loud enough so Lori can hear across the room where she pores over electronic records, books, stacks of paper, and files. Leslie remembers the unknown in that location from the year before.

Lori says she sees burial records with three babies called unknown fetus #3.

"Shit," Leslie says. That doesn't help. "We'll have to dig up all three."

The next 1960 case is a skull, found in December in an alley off Whittier Avenue. The ME's notes list it as a possible "negroid female."

"Man, wouldn't it be something if it was just sitting in evidence," Leslie says.

"We need to go to the medical examiner's office," Shannon adds, "because the head doesn't take up much space or need to be refrigerated, so it might still be there."

This decade is moving faster. In concert, they try to match police files with cemetery records. More potential adult matches are found. March 1961 has a third unknown fetus #3 in the cemetery records. It may match the police file of unknown fetus #3 found in a toilet by police officers. The bathroom was in the employment security commission office. The baby was delivered there and the mother left. The placenta and umbilical cord were still attached. They put it on the potential dig list.

The file for case #2310 is dated April 5, 1961. The report lists a bunch of bones found the day before.

"Male #1, unknown," Kelsey declares.

The air is silent for a moment as everyone seems to hope there might be more information volunteered from someone in the room. But there is not.

"Okay, keep rolling," Leslie says forcefully. They need to look for more information and the afternoon is beginning to display everyone's growing impatience.

There's more bad news. Kelsey tells her the homicide file is just a single page, no more.

"That's it, one page?" Leslie asks with disgust.

Leslie pulls out maps to the Garden of Prayer section at United Memorial. She is running the maps in her head and isn't sure if there is an unknown body in that section. They haven't dug there before.

The next baby is listed as "squashed" unknown fetus #6.

Two more don't seem to be homicides and they come off the list. The next is a Michigan State Police case, but they have only a skull. Another skull is a Wayne County case. The agencies might be able to add more.

Unknown baby #7 was found partially burned in an incinerator in the Wayne County jail.

"Likely a fetus they hid to protect a guard who impregnated an inmate," Shannon says.

Case 61-7526 is baby #20 found on Napoleon Street. An hour into the afternoon, they are mostly encountering files on babies; a stillborn White male found in a garbage can.

It might be harder to find a genetic match from a baby left to die.

"We know no one is looking for that baby," Shannon says bitterly. It grates on her. December 26, 1961, is unknown fetus #20 for the year.

Shannon is stressed and frequently popping open and downing Five-Hour Energy drinks. She can't take any more baby cases. "No more babies," she declares, visibly agitated. She tells everyone to step out of the 1960s and pick a new year. It is not a suggestion. They agree to go to the end of the list.

The file, dated April of 2009, indicates a jogger in Canton Township has found a femur, the thigh bone. They match the numbers to other files: NamUs file number # 11416 and a Canton police number 09-2404. A murder case perhaps, but not someone they can dig for.

The next 2009 file has been identified through other means as Richard Flint.

"He's a win," Leslie exclaims with a bit of glee, meaning he has won his own name back. A February 9, 2009, case starts as an unknown male, but the paperwork later identifies him as David Kopp. He died of hypothermia. They can delete the file from their list.

These more recent unsolved homicide cases move faster because they contain more details. They quickly determine that the file for December 4, 2008, is an unknown male buried in Knollwood, Angels row, section 529 D. The matching NamUS file is 11695. He died in a vacant apartment at 440 Peterboro St.

"NamUs records indicate this is a possible identification to Donald Harold Resko, White male," Lori calls out. The police file offers a birthdate of 2 November 1933 from a piece of identification found at the scene. The case was assigned originally to homicide detectives for some reason. Shannon needs to double check to verify that the case should be closed or whether they need to pull the body to obtain DNA. As expected, the day's work is creating more investigative work for Shannon.

Then comes the case of the dead guy who somehow ended up at the bottom of an elevator shaft that was flooded. There is the baby discovered when it fell from the ceiling at a funeral home. There is the man found in the field with two gunshot wounds to his right shoulder.

"Wait, I've got a position number," Lori yells. She has matched this case and several others to potential burial sites.

The next baby file sounds familiar to Kelsey.

"Is this already in blue?" Leslie asks, wondering if they have worked this file already and tried to dig for the body. They turn to each other. But when matching the information, it appears to be a different baby girl buried in Knollwood in 2011.

"We're oranging that one," Leslie says, indicating they would add it to the list of bodies to dig for.

Becca pulls out her orange highlighter.

File 07-11353 has six gunshot wounds and a missing head and hands, but the DNA is on file, so that comes off the list of potentials.

By 2:00 p.m., 19 orange markers jump from the sheets and another 25 cases have the word "delete" inked next to them. A few have been resolved by another agency or organization. Others are such small parts—the tip of a child's finger—that it's not likely to be a successful dig.

Having abandoned the earlier years at Shannon's request, they are working backwards through the last of 1993 and they know that the cases are getting tougher to solve as they get older. There will be less orange on the page.

Lots of the burials prior to 1993 are at United Memorial, where the markers, boxes, and ground are so much more challenging when trying to produce a successful dig. Bodies are buried deeper, the land has a high-water table, and the bodies aren't in concrete vaults.

And they are back to so many more babies.

Maybe it is just as well that Shannon is now preoccupied on her phone because dwelling on the cases would likely plunge her back into her morning funk. She is still responsible for missing persons cases every day, as well as several other tasks, including the duty to respond to officer-involved shootings. Two shootings in the morning have given way to a triple shooting just after lunchtime. Between text messages and emails, she's trying to find a missing file on a potential dig, one where a man's foot was found at the bottom of a river in a block of concrete.

By 3:00 p.m. the banter disappears as the list of ME and police files projected on the eight-foot-wide screen gives way to giant, closeup photos of baby remains found in dumpsters, sewers, and alleys. The black-and-white autopsy photos weren't part of the standard ME records in the earlier files. Sadness is heavy in the room. Some look away.

The baby death marked as #1971 has massive body trauma, with pictures that verify the baby was in a bag, tossed, and then likely run over by a car. The details limit any assumptions about the critical location information. Sometimes cemeteries drop unidentified babies into the same space as an unidentified adult, laying them at the adult's feet. It's not allowed, but it's done.

By 4:00 p.m. Shannon has lost the phone message war and left the room to the four remaining women, at least temporarily.

For the nearly one hundredth time, someone reads gruesome details in a monotone voice from the next file aloud: "Woman found an arm hanging on a nail in her garage."

They know they are nearing the end of the day, so they must get through the remaining files. It has taken so much time to coordinate their schedules. They won't have a chance to get this group of women together again soon.

Someone reads: "Baby found in box behind cemetery, potential abrasions on side of head, death likely asphyxia." As a group, they agree to pass. Perhaps it is just exhaustion kicking in from the up and down, adrenaline-filled day. They agree there is no evidence of severe trauma. No one ruled the case a homicide. Instead, the baby was placed in a box and dropped off in a cemetery.

Shannon returns.

They are collectively reasoning aloud to help get through it as if it will propel them to the day's end faster.

"I don't think anybody's looking for that baby," somebody says.

"Nobody's looking for any of these babies," another adds.

"Yeah, but it's not a clear-cut murder," Shannon says.

Now, nearly all the remaining two dozen or so cases are from the early 1960s, and the information is limited. Babies are described in one, two, or three-page reports. Shannon's pile of cases calling for further investigation has grown, and those baby cases may never be solved.

No one is looking for any of these people anymore. They must be the ones to do it. All the women are thinking it, but they can't share their conversation aloud. There just isn't time.

The long day is ending with the same dreary winter weather that escorted everyone to the building at daybreak. More lines on the Excel sheet have been highlighted with orange. The projector's off button is pushed. They begin to clean up the day's trash of food wrappers, abandoned paper notes, energy shot containers, and more. Pens, papers, laptops, and water bottles go back into boxes, and Leslie's team takes the precious paper posters off the wall to roll up.

They take stock of the project's successes to date. They have received word that they have a DNA match for a half dozen previous digs, including Anita Wiley. They have more than two dozen sets of bones acquired for potential DNA analysis if they can get them to a lab. Today they have found 19 cold case homicides they are ready to try to find in a cemetery.

With winter frost still a possibility, they know that the day's work won't result in digging for months. Till then, Shannon hopes Leslie will find the needed funding and Leslie hopes Shannon will recruit the right mix of available people and materials for the digs.

It's been a sad but successful day.

CHAPTER 21

Grimace and Cheetos

Karen, one of the team leaders, walks her team to their first dig site. Their task is to stand by and wait. They have been assigned an excavator and operator, Brian, who carefully maneuvers his big rig over to the team's first dig location.

With the precision honed by his years of working around utility lines, Brian delicately stretches out and positions the teeth of the bucket. It's his first strike of the day, and it's just moments after 9:00 a.m. A pink card secured to a wooden 1 x 2-inch stake guides his placement above the grass that has finally turned green from the summer rain and sun.

The teeth move one inch into the ground, preparing for the first swipe back toward his cab. By manipulating the four main control levers, he swiftly peels back slightly more than six feet of what looks like fresh rolled sod in one motion. It's the beginning of what will likely be eight hours in the black leather seat. So far, so good. The team leader tells him to keep going. He is looking for a pine coffin below. But more dirt needs to come off first and all of it needs to be neatly stacked beside the hole so it can be put back at some point. He needs to go down several feet but still be wary of hitting and damaging the top of a concrete vault.

Methodically, Brian scoops up some deep brown Michigan earth. Rocks and torn apart grass pieces come along with it as Brian empties the bucket onto a huge, bright blue tarp beside the deepening hole.

Once his initial work is done, they'll move a tent over to cover the site and obscure any views from prying eyes in the air, whether news media planes or drone cameras—another lesson learned from the 2019 dig. Shannon is particularly sensitive to who is watching. Early on, news cameras caught caskets being lifted out and put beside holes. Disturbed family members of loved ones in caskets "in the way" of the intended targets sued the city. There is no other way to exhume a body that is three or four caskets down. It doesn't make it more pleasant or otherwise matter that a court order allows the moving of caskets to exhume someone below. Or what remains of a casket.

Seven PPE-clad members of Karen's team hover around, silver duct tape sealing their white coveralls to their yellow boots and blue gloves. Some hold the four assigned long-handled shovels. The tarps are covering several gravesites with copper-looking headstones that were long ago set into the ground. Some of the markers identify grandmothers, or fathers. Above and below ground, they wait.

The team will work together for the week and the first day is a bit of a reunion for some and a get-to-know-each-other for the rest. Two of Jodi's students are on Karen's team, their youth concealed from distinction by their Tyvek. The students are quiet, but the experienced FBI agents, Detroit police officers, and others exchange curriculum vitae while they wait their turn. Where did you go to school? What offices have you worked in? Is this your first dig?

The team's large purple flag is planted into the ground nearby to let Shannon, Leslie, and others know which team is working at what location. The flag will move with the team as their assignment on the ground changes. The purple team is called Grimace—the color of the large, purple anthropomorphic and stone-faced mascot created as a McDonald's restaurant character in the 1990s. It is prescient for the expressions seen on the faces of the many workers throughout the day. It's a slow process demanding the patience to stand and remain silent until they are called.

Each team has a color and a nickname. Not far away, the yellow Big Bird team has already broken ground. Far across the cemetery, the red Elmo team, the teal Aquaman team, and the navy-blue Gonzo team have excavations underway. The orange Cheetos team is somewhere, too. The names encourage a bit of a silly release that Leslie knows comes from the stress of the first day in the three scheduled dig days. July is the first dig of the season. Any water they encounter cannot be as bad as that first May dig. The water table in Michigan is so high they may as well have been in scuba gear instead of Tyvek. Every year, they learn from their mistakes.

"You each get your own excavator this year and you will each get your own water pump," Leslie announces to all at the Bone Tent. "You'll get a generator for each team and 100 feet of discharge hose."

It's still a wet business, but not as bad as May and June. The pumps and hoses will help draw the water from in and around the decomposing boxes and bodies. Lots of water all but ensures the first visible coffins will crumble at the touch. The teeth on Brian's buckets are close, so very close to the vault. Can he balance them in just the right spot and avoid breaking a concrete vault top or upending the brittle wooden box with the skeletal remains down just a few inches deeper? All eyes are glued to the tiniest movement of the excavator. Several faces cringe involuntarily as the powerful metal teeth gingerly maneuver against their target.

Even when the ground is open, there is no assurance they are in the right spot. These markers signify the educated guesses of Leslie, Shannon, Lori, and, most importantly, the cemetery staff. But they must do it this way. Cemeteries that look so neat above ground are complicated underground. Tree roots, shifting and settling ground, collapsing pine boxes, and, oh yes, the water table that shifts seemingly everything millimeters here and inches there. Michigan is surrounded by the largest supply of fresh water in the world—the five Great Lakes—and homeowner wells can be as shallow as 25 feet to get drinkable water.

At each dig site, finding the box is an essential step and they look at every piece of information Shannon has gathered to be sure they are about to dig for a murder victim. Perhaps it is evidence of murder with a bullet mark that has nicked a clavicle, or a blood-stained hat that is with the corpse.

With enough dirt removed, those surrounding Brian look for the two steel eyebolts secured to the top of the box. They reach in with foot-long steel hooks and attach the chains. The links are half-inch-thick and two inches long. They help slip hooks and chains into each, allowing Brian to slowly loosen the top of the two-thousand-pound concrete box. As he lifts it, a distinctive whiff of death escapes in all directions. The lid teeters a bit, but Brian's skilled hands allow him to steady his payload quickly, preventing it from bumping into and cracking the side of the vault or the top. Either would be a significant setback in time. Dangling, the top moves up a few more inches. When it is a foot or so above ground, Brian gingerly shifts the lid over to the newly created pile of dirt.

Now the hard work begins. Karen's team is looking for the person on the pink tag. Cemetery records indicate the remains will be the third box down. Precision and patience will be necessary to respectfully disinter those in the way of their target casket. The unnamed people here are buried with named individuals who may have a nameplate on the ground above. When the county buries its bodies, they bury several at a time to save money.

Mixed in with the unidentified murdered victims are people buried with their true names, whether Bill Johnson or Sally Williams. They are in the paupers' section simply because they died when their families weren't around or when the family could not afford a burial. Still, those boxes have names on them. It seems wrong to disturb those caskets with a name, but even to make that observation is a bit of a slap in the face to people buried without a name.

Karen's team is fortunate. Their hole is not filled with too much water. Across the cemetery, another team is fighting lower ground and has found their skeletons are in caskets swimming in murky, smelly water. Their discharge hose is stretched out 100 feet in a direction where no stakes with pink cards foretell a hopeful dig spot for the day. The hose is hooked to a generator and eagle-eyed workers are sucking out what they hope is only water from the hole. The chance of pulling out an intact casket looks increasingly slim.

Nearby, donated orange Home Depot paint buckets are filled with supplies each team might need. Another team leader is waiting for Jodi to stop by and muster all her skills to find the right bones that may net some DNA. Even when it's dry, it's a challenge. The year before, team members could stack two boxes on top of each other for support at one dig, a sign of dry boxes. Not really today since the boxes are too soggy and might collapse into one another.

Jodi walks towards the water filled casket. She juggles a radio in one hand and a pen in another. In the nook of her elbow, she is cradling a clipboard made of aluminum with a 9 x 12 x 1 inch storage box attached that opens with a flip of the lid. She is dressed in Tyvek, too. Not expecting to go into a hole, the top half of her suit is not yet pulled up and taped, and the extra gloves for the day are inside a plastic bag secured with two strips of gray duct taped just above her left knee.

She reaches into the far end of one box. She seems unaware that just inches beyond her foot, the flat copper headstone memorializes the "wife and mother" Doris, buried in 2001. It is not a day to be overly sentimental.

In her element, her hands move as if she was looking for a matching sock in her dresser drawer. She pulls out one bone. Not the right one. Then another. No, not that. Then another. This one has the white "stuff" that is the consistency of papier mâché smeared all over it. The goo adheres to her gloves, her pants, and anything else it touches. She has more reasons than the pandemic to wear a plastic face shield. They know the technical name for this stage of decomposition but rarely use it when someone can just say it is covered in goop. She gingerly inserts the bone in a clear plastic bag that looks like a Ziplock freezer bag for leftovers. The bag has been marked with the details of the case before it is sealed for future access by someone in a lab sometime in the future.

When water and bacteria are present, bodies are more likely to decay, sometimes producing adipocere, a waxy or soap-like substance referred to as corpse wax or grave wax. Many of them just call it goop. This process is called saponification, a process that turns body fat into adipocere.

This day, the humidity is rising with the temperature and Leslie and Shannon are riding between teams in golf carts, sucking down bottles of water. The year before it was 95 degrees. A few samples have made their way to the Bone Tent. Lori is escorting and keeping track of the need for Jodi and other forensic anthropologists. Shannon's goal for this dig effort is 25 matching sets of bones. Sets of bones are needed because the protocol for this dig is that any forensic anthropologist is asked to find two different bones from each body. That improves the odds of finding DNA and allows samples to be sent to different labs, if needed. Twenty-five unidentified murder victims are on the court order, but Shannon has done the paperwork to prepare for many more if the digs go quickly and she can expand the court order.

They took out 26 sets of bones from Knollwood the year before, Leslie notes, so she is a bit surprised when Shannon settles on 25 for the dig. They both know that Leslie and her other resources may not be available in the future, so they are working as efficiently as possible.

This is just a process for Leslie. There is little she hasn't seen. When asked by a volunteer what she expects will happen when a vault is open, she explains in one long run-on sentence as if it will occur in minutes, not hours.

"Sometimes you pull up a four pack and the dead guy you want is number four so you have to bounce up one, two, and three, and hopefully there is a tag that survives, and you can unzip the bag and start fishing around for the bag of organs that they shove back into the cavity and sometimes you can tell if it is male or female." She pauses and adds, "Cemeteries hate it."

She pauses to watch Karen's team at work. They are finally in the right vault and need to get down to the third casket. Team members carefully position straps around the bottom of the first light brown wooden casket to maneuver it up and out of the vault. They are going to take the box up. The two men leave to decontaminate their entire body suits. Another team member sits on the students' side holding chains. They hook all the chains together. The first box seems solid and comes out of the hole intact and is set on top of another person's gravestone. The name on the box's tag makes it a bit too personal, as the accompanying foul smell leaves a brackish taste in the mouths of everyone nearby.

The digger starts and the big bucket is swung over the water-filled hole to try to pick up the second box. The chains are positioned but the D ring slides along the chain. It isn't tight enough. Despite the danger of getting hit by the bucket, a team member jumps in the hole and grabs the chain by hand. Brian takes the cue and moves ever so slightly again and again to make the chain taught. "You can do it," they encourage Brian, yelling over the sound of the excavator.

It takes most of an hour, but suddenly the second box is up and stacked near the first, perched not far from the pile of dirt on the blue tarp. The smell of the hole intensifies. They are surrounded by two bodies in broken boxes they don't need to get into, but instead need to get around.

"There is a name plate over here," someone yells about the next box down. "Tag," another yells, literally meaning he has located the tag. He reads aloud, "unknown male. Think we found him." They recognize immediately that the darkened wooden top indicates more severe deterioration. It has been shattered into pieces by the years, water, and weight of the first boxes. Whether it can be moved is in the hands of the team working together with straps to lift it from the vault.

Jodi stops to see her students, handing out pictures and a stick to use to keep gloves clean. "You need to take pictures of the dental arches," she tells them. "Look at the dental photos in the autopsy," she urges. "Can you see photos of the teeth?" The radio crackles again. A forensic anthropologist is needed at another site. Lori whisks Jodi towards the location, her floppy hat waving with the movement of the golf cart.

As the morning hours fade, Karen's team is still looking for their first success. The yellow team has moved to a third site, or is it the red team? It's not a competition, they remind themselves. Teams are tagging out to get water and face their most daunting task of every day, finding a way to go to the bathroom while wrapped head to toe like a hermetically sealed loaf of bread.

Those in charge of the Bone Tent have a handful of successes already. But it's lunch time now. Everyone breaks at nearly the same time. There are few opportunities to sit down while they are working, so lunch provides a needed respite. Sandwiches, chips, cookies, pop, and water are on the menu. It's pop because they are in Michigan to dig. If they were in the south, it would be Coke. And in the northeast and southwest it would be soda. But today they are firmly in pop territory.

At lunch, they speak a bit about their successes and frustrations of the day but more of their families, friends, and work back home. If they can, many lower the top half of their hot Tyvek body suit, revealing sweat-soaked t-shirts underneath. Some proudly wear black Operation UNITED t-shirts. On the back are some of the key agencies, Detroit Police, NamUs, FBI Detroit, MSP. They intermingle with the volunteers who aren't used to lunching with police and FBI agents. Skilled investigators and evidence collectors in the group forget that the secrets of their talents are a curiosity. The outsiders ask about training and advice for their own kids who want to go into law enforcement.

Sprinkles of rain encourage urgency and no one lingers under the tent.

Somewhere around the operation's fifth hour, Karen's team is ready to lift the third casket from the vault. With the lid off the vault, dirt is dumping in, and water begins to accumulate. "Put those face masks on," she yells, offering a frightening risk. "It's slopping around, and you don't want that in your mouth. The whole thing will be filled with water."

Diggers are standing on the side of the vault, leaning on their shovels when not scooping dirt. As their boots begin to sink, they begin pumping water out and someone jumps in to clear mud. "Get a bucket down there so we're not scooping the dirt twice," someone says encouragingly.

Now a crowbar is the preferred tool. If they can pop off the center board of the coffin's top, they can see if there is a body bag that can be pulled out.

"See if you can unzip it," the team leader directs.

It's nearly noon and finally a body bag is visible, covered in mud and water.

"If we do that, isn't it going to get more water in it?" comes the reply from several feet down.

Maybe we can move the body and put a line in to drain some of the water," another suggests. They suck out more water from the inside of the box and the vault.

This body was buried in 2011 and was wearing a winter coat. They need a better view. Someone pops the third board from the top. If they can find a zipper, they will search for the bones while the bag is inside the box.

"You need a finger," the team lead asks one of Jodi's students who is taking her turn in the hole. "Yes, I do," the student says, tipping her face skyward from four feet down in the hope that she is tall enough. The team lead bends down to push the student's glasses back up the bridge of her nose.

"I'm sure there is water in that bag," the team lead says as she hands a pair of scissors down. "Let's open it and see what's inside."

"Should I cut along the zipper line," the student asks?

"Cut anywhere," another team members macabrely chimes in. "you can't hurt him." It's a good thing Leslie and Shannon are not nearby to hear the bones cry out.

Inside, the body sits in water. The students switch places. The one jumping from the hole is a bit weak-kneed. "You're not going to faint, are you?" she hears. "No," she replies.

The bag is soup inside.

"You may have to hand parts out," the team leader says. "It looks like connective tissue."

They call for the forensic anthropologist. It begins to rain. The sprinkles cool things off a bit.

Team members move a pre-staged blue tent over the open grave and wait. Just 20 feet away, a stick with a pink ribbon is pelted by the rain. Below is a person buried in 2008 after their body was found face down in a water-filled elevator shaft of an abandoned building.

No luck yet on the bones. Discussion ensues about whether to pull the box out. Thunder roars a bit too close. Others jump in to prepare the box for removal. The mud they are hand scooping is grey, not like the fertile brown topsoil. The body bag is visible, but it is covered with mud and the collapsed wall.

Leverage from the shovel releases the suction-grip imposed by the mud and the pine box frees from the box below. With the help of two chains wrapped around it, it is lifted out. Water pours from the box back into the vault and onto the surrounding grass. The pine box smell mixes with the smell of the ground and decay.

"It's crazy to think this guy was buried," Brian says, his face whitening as he registers that his water drenched load carries a real body.

At another dig site, students perk up as their professor arrives at their site to fish for bones. She likes the cuboids from the feet, she explains. They are usually big enough to provide an assured DNA sample.

"African American male with a beard," she says, as the left clavicle is pulled from the bag. That's usually easier to find.

"Look at how beautiful his smile is," she says, always seeing the person alive and having a conversation with him. The information on another murder victim indicates he was buried with a beige and teal sweatshirt, blue pajama pants, and a black jacket with white stripes. She is non plussed about the other autopsy details: homicide, burned, and found behind a closet door that was held closed by a cord.

"That's called homicide," she says to the students. He was 140 pounds and 6 foot 1, so he's folded in the box at the bottom. His age is marked from 60 to 85.

"Once you figure out where the feet are..." she is explaining to nearby students as the person's bones are bagged and tagged and headed to the bone tent. But just as quickly she is gone. There is a problem at the Elmo location. The baby they are looking for is in a grave that is all soup.

Dustin arrives to shoot the pictures. "Jodi says to do a full dental and says you'll know what that means," someone tells him.

The rain has leaked down into the boxes that were lifted out to get to the target coffin. The gravel and pothole filled roads are now muddy water hazards to walkers.

Now, they need to verify they have found the right body. Each person is a crime victim and sometimes that means finding the skull first to find the expected bullet hole or two, or perhaps a snapped neck or severed mandible. In her metal clipboard box Shannon has provided, Karen reviews the few details discovered. Some files have dental records that make it easier to look for a person with missing or crowned teeth. This man was buried in a tweed jacket. Some personal possessions were buried with him. A quick survey assures them their findings are true.

It's finally Karen's time to call out on the radio for the help of a forensic anthropologist. Excitement fills the air, despite the even more nauseating smell about to be unleashed. But first, Jodi needs to finish her work with the Aquaman team. So, they wait.

"OK, buddy," Jodi says, talking directly to the bones she is fishing through. She looks back at the paperwork. "This guy was huge. This is the strangest autopsy I've ever seen. Oh my gosh, whoever was doing the autopsy cut the whole breast plate." She reaches in to find two different bones and pairs them together for one successful search. She lifts off the entire breast plate, necessitating that she put it back.

"Look at the skull," she exclaims in surprise.

“Oh my gosh,” her student says, leaning in further over the box. “Where is the top of his head?”

While they await Jodi’s arrival, the Grimace team begins digging their next grave. The tags all indicate known buries, Edith, LeMont, Laverne, so they are in the wrong spot. But still, it helps future digging. They realize they are next door to the body they need and soon they are making progress on their second body.

The wait seems interminable.

Finally, Jodi appears, laughing and talking to everyone. Jodi is a shining light wherever she goes and unknowingly compels those around her to listen and watch her every move. She is ever the teacher and says aloud what she is doing. The team huddles nearby, surrounded by the remnants of broken casket number three, “unknown male,” and gives her room to zip the body bag open.

Like a skilled surgeon, she reaches into the bag. Bigger bones favor a positive DNA finding. Jodi particularly likes ankle bones. She knows each bone by its touch—femur, phalanges, clavicle, cuboid, scapula, metatarsal, sternum, tibia. She hardly needs to look down as her hand skillfully reaches around in the bag, up, then down, then up again. Skeletons might start out looking like a Halloween decoration, but the comparison quickly disappears when water enters the box, the ground shifts, and decomposition and other factors come into play. Clothes on a body can help keep the bones in place.

It takes her only minutes—ten at most—to find what she needs. She tries for a tarsal bone—maybe a cuboid—from the bottom half of the body, and a clavicle from the top half, taking one from each side of the body. She pulls the bones out and drops them into a waiting evidence bag. The bag is sealed, marked, and sent off to the Bone Tent.

It’s very anticlimactic. We don’t know if the DNA extraction will be successful, whether a DNA match can be found for the unidentified murder victim, and if that might solve a crime. Either way and even if it takes years, once testing is complete the team intends to return the bones to their final resting place to keep the person in one grave.

Now, they must reverse the process, finding a way to place back into the open vault the caskets that are lying beside the vault. It's hopeless with the damaged second box and they call for boards to re-secure the top of the casket. Forensic television shows glamorize all this, but real life is not lost to the participants. Foul smelling mud is smeared on everyone's clothes, shoes, and more. No one wants to think of what is in the mud. It takes an hour or more, but Brian, Karen, and the team manage to close the site back up, save the grass carpet.

They still have time to try to find the body at that second site.

CHAPTER 22

The Last Baby

Radios announce news of another find.

At still another location, they have pulled a partial skull and mandible out and placed them on a blue tarp. The six or seven white teeth displayed are a sharp contrast to the bone that has that brownish gray hew of decaying wood. A photographer is on his knees, his gloved hands wrapped around his black FBI-issue Nikon. His mask-covered face is an equidistant handful of inches from the jawbone and the grass. Once they open a grave, Leslie explains, they want to get anything not already in the investigative file. They will avoid going back down again, if possible.

Other teams are doing well, which is good because it looks like the sprinkles will give way to real rain soon. The Grimace team's new site is more forgiving, but as the afternoon hours reduce to a short supply, another team has hit a perhaps insurmountable snag.

Lori and Shannon have on their list the hope of finding a murdered baby. Looking for babies is its own challenge. At United Memorial, Babyland is the first place to look. But at Knollwood, it's more of a crap shoot. Prior owners faced several legal actions for improper burial practices, including many babies not being buried on time and others buried improperly.

But Lori is the expert on the Knollwood records. And today, she believes the missing baby they want to find has been buried in a quite disturbing place. Lori believes the murdered baby was warehoused for the rest of eternity on the same day a man was buried by the county. To save costs, she believes the baby's body might have been slipped into the man's casket—left to eternity some place near his bare feet.

Baby murders. There's a special place in hell for people who kill babies.

But no one at the cemetery can think about that now. Good police work demands that emotion be set aside. The team digging for the baby is simply a group of professionals carrying out their duties. The murdered baby is a person and deserves to be found.

Lori's best calculation is that the murdered baby might be found in a shared casket located further west in the cemetery. The identity of the baby's potential bunk mate is known, but the county buried him in the same fashion because there was no money or family available. He has a name, and the burial teams say it aloud with great respect. "We believe the baby is possibly at the feet" of Mr. So-and-So, one team member says. But if his soul is listening, the buried man might be crying now. Surely, he thought, his burial was the last of what must have been many indignities that led him to this final resting place. But if his spirit can detect it, he is in for so much more before today's sun sets.

The team is "popping up his casket," as Leslie would say. Mr. So-and-So—we'll call him Joe Dan Smith—is unfortunately intertwined with the day's objectives. A 79-year-old White male buried in the 1950s. While the color-coded teams continue to work toward their final successes of the day, the baby-hunters get underway. Lori has pinpointed Joe Dan Smith's location, and the grass and dirt is moved with relative ease from the golf-course-looking patch of land, smack in the middle of their digging area. It could be quick—but it is not.

The grave is filled with water. No problem. Pump, hose, drain, wait, repeat. Joe Dan Smith's box is located as the water level seems to recede. Women may lead, but sometimes the men's strength helps with pulling big chains across a box to hook it up to supports on the excavator. As each box is lifted out, the winds before the storm move across the open ground. The cool air is welcome, but it brings with it the unmistakable smell of death disturbed.

"It's weird you can't see anything, it's legitimately soup," anyone could have said, but Sue did say. They are pumping water out at the rate of an inch every one minute from around the coffin with a goal to lift the body bag out and put it on a board. "Find me a baby," Sue declares as the crew pries off the last top board. But his casket, too, is filled with water. Worse, the bag inside Joe Dan Smith's the casket is filled with water. Everyone within earshot hears the radio call seeking direction. They smell the rain coming, as anyone in Michigan understands.

Police and medical examiner reports note the ten-inch-long baby was put into a 30-inch, Size 1 body bag, shortly after it was found in a bag in the street in 1999. Certain factors help medical examiners determine whether a baby died by natural causes or manmade. For example, the fetus may have an umbilical cord around its neck or be wrapped in a sheet or blanket. A baby born alive and abandoned will have signs that oxygen entered their lungs. A malnourished baby has signs of stunted growth both in weight and height.

The team looking for the baby is waiting for an anthropologist, but there aren't enough to go around. Sue is in the bag trying to determine if they have the right body. "It might be a woman. If it is, we are in the wrong box," she reports up, asking for more information. "Was it a big man with those big joints?" Is he big and tall or big and fat?" Trying to problem solve before forensic anthropologist Meredith gets there, Sue theorizes, "We might have to tarp that guy out" or abandon the search.

Jodi is not yet at Sue's dig site, but her course of direction is firm.

"No matter," Jodi says, "every individual is unique and deserves to be identified, even if only a DNA profile that will remain without a name or a life history until they are found, perhaps by future generations searching their family genealogy." Shannon and Leslie began their odyssey with a goal to reveal every family member's final chapter.

But Jodi's reason for being out in the grass this day is personal in a different way.

"To those who ask," she explains, haltingly. "Giving them a name … Connecting them to family …" Her eyes wander as if she'll see the right words in the sky only with sufficient concentration. "To let someone know where their loved one is … That's crucial," she adds with finality.

Her speech is generally quick and modulated, making the last bit sound so uncharacteristic. She can't find the right words or words with enough meaning to explain why these digs are so important to her.

But then she does.

"I was 28 years old," she begins. "I was in a motor vehicle accident and had a closed head injury and lost my entire episodic memory."

The car accident took away all her early memories, permanently. Yes, just like in the movies, she explains. Only this really happened. She doesn't volunteer it, but she doesn't hide it either.

She's become a little rusty at explaining the whole ordeal. She initially offers snippets to satisfy the curious and explains for the thousandth time what episodic memory is: explicit, long-term memories such as where you attended first grade, who is your favorite person you dated, or where you were when the September 11, 2001, terrorist attacks occurred.

"I lost .. yes, the whole first 28 .. I would say, OK, the first 30 years of my life, because I didn't really start making new memories until eight or nine months after the accident, and then they are patchy until a couple of years in. So, I really started university when I was two, so you know, when I was 30.

It's why her beloved overstuffed office of books and mementos shows few signs of a lifetime of memories. Though Jodi has dedicated her life to finishing the stories of those who have been silenced, in a bit of cruel irony, her own story will never be finished.

"I just never grew up. I don't have any memories the others have," she says, explaining that over many months, her medical team reintroduced her to the idea of what living on Earth truly means. "By the time I was making new memories, they'd already introduced my parents to me as my parents, and my brother as my brother, and my kids as my kids. If they had given me six kids and said, 'These are your kids,' I would have said, 'Okay.' I wouldn't have any children if the woman who had my body before me hadn't had those kids."

She's detached from that woman who used to live in her body, but is clearly grateful for the groundwork she laid. "The woman who had the body before me," as she calls her, "had a degree in business."

The accident changed her life trajectory in an unfathomable way. Her expression changes with a sudden realization. "I've not yet lived more years as this Jodi than the other Jodi." The Jodi she does not know was born halfway between Detroit and Buffalo, New York. She offers unsolicited clarity. "That's on the Canada side, as people in the area say." She only knows this, she explains unnecessarily, because she was told so.

Besides learning about episodic memory, she learned there are several types of memory, an inexact science itself. She came to understand some of what she was retaining was her own implicit, procedural memory. The motor skills she uses without thinking, such as tying shoes, playing a guitar, or juggling.

Whether she missed 30 years of her life, or a murdered baby survived only 30 hours after birth before freezing to death in a park, each life must be accounted for, she stresses. Her own recovery, and the science behind it, allowed her to make sense of what happened, even when it made her sad or frustrated. She wants that even for the babies. Science helped her comprehend how she could survive yet only retain seemingly random parts of that Canadian-born business graduate. She knows how to eat with a fork but doesn't know her own children.

"It's very difficult for me—I mean, I'm much better now—but you know it's very difficult for me to know what's learned versus what people innately know. I have all this functional memory that's not connected to anything.

"I didn't realize that humans couldn't just type on a keyboard," she says. "I had no idea that you had to learn to do that. I couldn't teach my kids to drive because I had never learned. But yet, I drive. There are all kinds of things that I can do. Like knitting. I didn't know that you had to learn to knit. I just know how to do things."

Although she is in a challenging field of work, it is the accident that helped her get there. The accident injured her left temporal lobe, leaving her aphasic, unable to express or understand speech.

"My brain swelled up inside my skull and my cerebral spinal fluid came out my nose and out my ear and you know that sort of thing," she says in a clinical tone. "I wasn't able to talk and then when I did speak, even though I knew what I was saying, it was just blah, blah, blah to others."

When therapists began telling her she needed to adjust to her disability, and people began to speak to her as if she wasn't smart enough to understand, Jodi says she was so angry she took matters into her own hands.

"I decided I was gonna go to university and show everybody there was nothing wrong with my brain," she says, laughing a bit as she confesses how she managed to get into Western University in Ontario. "I used the grades that 'the woman who had my body before me' got for her business degree. Talk about impostor syndrome."

To her, she was a two-year-old. With her only frame of reference being the medical personnel around her, her experiences prompted her to begin a course of study as an occupational therapist. But when the university discontinued the program, she had to find a new direction. Finding a new direction is quintessential Jodi Barta. She is often heard telling someone that the word "no" is just an invitation to find another way to do something.

She focused on the courses she enjoyed the most, anthropology and genetics, convincing the university to award her a Bachelor of Science degree in both. She has a big brain, she explains. "It's just the one that came with my head."

Her grades matched, and her work ethic led to tremendous academic success. Still in Canada, she earned a PhD from McMaster University and then did post-doctoral work at the University of Ontario. Her published research topics included methodological improvements for the extraction of ancient and forensic DNA, work on Roman cemetery populations, and fingerprint and blood impression analysis.

After a divorce, sans child support, she moved to the State of Washington determined to earn enough to take care of her children. She loved it on the West Coast, but when her grandmother asked her to move closer to home, she began applying for teaching and museum jobs back in Toronto, Ontario.

Serendipity led her to Madonna University in Livonia when her son enrolled there on a soccer scholarship. He had taken some sciences classes and called her. "You must come fix these," he compelled her. Just as she was considering accepting a job in Canada, Madonna posted the position of Director of Forensic Sciences. Much of her studies and work had focused on DNA extraction and her anthropology expertise made her a hot candidate for the open job. Her son was at Madonna, and that was the deciding factor.

"It all worked perfectly," she said. At Madonna, unlike at larger research institutions, she said, she is able to work with less red tape and "get shit done faster." It's a byproduct of having to start her life over. She doesn't have time to waste.

So yes, looking for the baby in a soup bag of bones is required. It's her way of showing that no one should be forgotten. It's hard to look for an adult in a grave in Michigan, let alone a baby. Decomposing bodies go through various stages that are dependent, mostly on exposure to moisture, heat, and bacteria. Childhood fears or fascination with mummies comes without the understanding, for example, that mummification requires heat or wind or something else that will dry out a body. In the watery world of Michigan, decomposition moves in the opposite direction.

Doctors hunting for the clavicle or tarsal bone must squeeze out the toothpaste-like substance to see if they have found their pot of gold. Jodi says it clinically: “It depends on how saponified the body is, which means how much grave wax is present, because sometimes you have to disarticulate the body.”

She means that, at times, you need to pull the bone joints apart.

While the faint at heart take the opportunity to step away and steady their stomachs, Jodi’s impenetrable armor allows her to contemplate her next move.

CHAPTER 23

Joe Dan Smith

Together they stand beside the hole Joe Dan Smith once filled. From a distance, it might be mistaken as a funeral burial celebration of life. But what surrounds them is the futility of the day. A car-sized blue tarp is piled with grass and dirt on one side. A red pump sits beside it with 100 feet of hose stretched out. Once engorged with grave water, it is now flattened. Shovels and rakes are spread across the grass, some leaning on the idled excavator.

The team pulls two caskets out and set them aside. It's clear why Shannon, Leslie, and Lori must plot out the digs for the day. It's bad enough they are working on top of dozens of marked and unmarked graves. They can't have teams working on top of each other, too.

They have found Joe Dan Smith, but the baby bones they need are elusive. Inside Joe Dan Smith's body bag, the content has been reduced to bones floating in soup. As the day nears its end, everyone is covered in soup from the protective suits they will peel off, down to the shoes that eventually mar the floor mats of their cars with goop. It's a sickening thing to think about if they let their minds wander while driving. But for now, they all need to keep their armor up.

They have been waiting an hour for one of the anthropologists to come to the red tent to look for bones. Finally, near 3 p.m., Jodi and Meredith join Sue to provide their advice on next steps. Sue begins, pointing to the body bag of bones and liquid. "This is…," she says as if introducing him at a summer bar-b-cue, "a delightful man but not relevant."

"I'm sorry," Meredith says with sincerity, addressing the deceased by name. The red team has not been able to find the baby so far and

"My working theory now," Sue explains, is that maybe the baby is in the grave next to this person, where another man is buried.

Searching inside the bag is not working. There are plenty of bones, but it's difficult to tell if a small bone is from a baby or from Joe Dan Smith. The dig team awaits instructions while Shannon, Leslie, Lori, and Jodi join in the debate.

The rain is coming.

"Pour 'em out," someone says. Some hesitate to be sure they understand. "Pour 'em out and make the skeleton." A quick glance of understanding passes across the group and then haste takes over. The largest blue tarp available is put beside Joe Dan Smith's casket. The bag is pulled and stretched over the tarp on one side. Together, team members unzip the body bag, open it, and pour Joe Dan Smith out in the direction of the open surface.

Bones and liquid rush from the bag. Gravity efficiently pulls the soup across the blue plastic in small rivers before slipping off the edge and seeping into the grass. They catch the edges to be sure no small bone pieces slip out of sight.

On hands and knees, expert fingers begin the process of picking up and manipulating bones to see if the Joe Dan Smith puzzle can be put together. They begin to pull one bone at a time. An intact skull is a good start, fewer pieces to find. Mandible, check. The person doing it has a coworker occasionally putting an ice pack on his Tyvek suit. They'll rebury him in another bag, safe and sound.

They wave their hands over the top of the bones to spread them out as if they are mixing a deck of cards before gathering them up to deal poker hands. It's as Jodi described. All the bones are white. Some are easier to pluck from the mess: ribs, sternum, scapula. The shape of cervical, thoracic, and lumbar vertebrae helps locate some or most of the spine. Time will tell. About 80 of the body's 206 bones are in the head and chest area, and it's harder to pull out all the smaller bones from the arms, legs, hands, and feet.

The rain had slowed as soon as it started, but now sprinkles begin to fall, and the anatomy test begins. Each foot has 26 bones. A hand has 27. The baby was only days or weeks old; no one can remember or has time to re-check the file again. Babies have as many as 300 different bones, several that fuse together as they grow. The size of the bones won't be measurably different. If two bodies are in the mix, they should be seeing some bones that don't seem to fit into the puzzle that is Joe Dan Smith.

The bones of Joe Dan Smith come together to show arms and hands, and then legs and feet begin to emerge. The effort is like a class exam. As Dan Joe Smith's white bones come into view like a rudimentary Halloween decoration on the blue tarp, they are still not finding bones that look like they could be from a baby.

Lori was reasonably convinced they had the right grave. No one wants to dig up Joe Dan Smith or anyone else for no reason. Bodies from the morgue are buried in groups and if the baby and Joe Dan Smith were buried the same day, it seems likely the baby should be there, too. Still, they are not seeing signs of the baby. A skillful team member continues to identify every bone located.

Jodi offers a different explanation. Maybe they will never find the bones because the baby's bones were so small, so porous, that they simply disintegrated. Audible sighs blending surprise and exasperation come from those who are hearing the theory about babies for the first time. It's as if the baby never existed.

They'll have to try another tack tomorrow. For now, everyone needs to rally to get this cemetery closed and shift their operation in reverse. Someone is rolling up the drain hose, knowing it will be used tomorrow. Grave water and soup drip from the end as it is coiled. Equipment is hauled across to be locked up in trailers. Every site worked on must have GPS coordinates taken to help with future digs since bones removed must eventually be replaced when returned from the lab.

A new body bag is requested so everyone can quickly scoop the remains into it, leading to another unavoidable indignity for Joe Dan Smith.

He is packed back into his new home and then into his damaged but salvageable casket. The remains on the blue tarp are shoveled and poured back into a new body bag and into the cavity where Joe Dan Smith's casket came from. One of the excavator operators working on that side of the cemetery climbs into his seat to finish the job. Shannon and Leslie have released most of the others for the day, but this gentleman is a full-time employee at the cemetery and very skilled in moving about their charges. He manipulates the caskets back into the ground and slides the dirt, scoop-by-scoop, into the hole. Around him, tired team members use rakes and shovels to fill the hole and smooth out the ground. It will settle over the next year and leave a divot if they don't mound the dirt up on the site.

The tent has been packed; the tools need to be washed down. The cleanup and decontamination crew is waiting for these last stragglers. Everyone who is suited up must return to the decontamination crew before being dismissed for the day. As one would do when dressing and undressing a child, an HMRT team member reverses the morning ritual, first spraying down the outside of each person. Then they carefully cut away the tape and peel off gloves. The top of the Tyvek suit is peeled all the way down to the yellow booties. They cut the binding around the ankles and pull the suit away. All are discarded in pop-up trash barrels. The same crew uses fire hoses to wash down the shovels, rakes, and other equipment used that day.

First on the scene, last to leave. Leslie and Shannon survey the successes of the day and plot out what the teams will look for the next morning. Each dig is a three-day dig event, and they want to take advantage of every hour with team members. They may never be able to get this large of a group together again. A cloud hangs over them as the realization is ever present that these digs are likely the only opportunity they will ever orchestrate to both give these murder victims back their names and maybe hold a murderer accountable.

A steady rain has begun. With goop still all over their boots, they climb into their cars to drive home. They need to be ready for tomorrow.

CHAPTER 24

The Numbers Game

Each year becomes easier than the last. Each dig week is less stressful than the last. Leslie begins assigning the same people to lead teams. She knows them, and they know each other's capabilities, and how to work with the spirit and soul of the cemeteries.

As the cemeteries became pockmarked with evidence of past digs, Leslie and Shannon use simple math calculations to more accurately find where one vault ends and the next is located. They are avoiding unforced errors like the first years, when they simply dug up the wrong person. Hunts for the more recent murder victims means bodies are in easier to locate concrete vaults.

Finally, five years after Shannon first challenged Leslie to help her find the faces on her walls, their last dig will have exhausted Shannon's primary box of files. The cemetery grass is growing again. Leslie's tools have been put away. Her team has turned to other FBI priorities. Jodi is back teaching.

As Leslie's counterparts from other FBI offices depart, other dig volunteers return to their departments, universities, and offices. Excavator operators are again securing Detroit's electric and other infrastructure needs. The forensic anthropologists no longer have a field experiment waiting for their students. They will have to come up with other ways to continue to bring their programs to life.

The digs were a first-of-a-kind operation for the FBI, an organization that dates back more than 100 years. Many search teams have dug and found one or a few bodies left by criminals, and some have conducted exhumations in cemeteries, but never on this scale. From the start,

Leslie could not have know that in the end, this would be her largest and most successful leadership undertaking of her FBI career. Here each exhumation may be the key to identify a homicide victim and give them a chance to locate a potential murderer. They all confess that it's been a bit mind blowing. But, as always, good planning got them where they are.

"We had no playbook," Leslie notes, recalling the dozens of times her team has been called up through the years to help the FBI or local law enforcement handle a body or body part. Leslie's methodical ways have served her well to help keep the project funded, ensure that the right personnel are on scene, and to make sure the bosses in her Detroit office, at FBI headquarters, and the FBI Laboratory are happy.

Several law enforcement agencies from across the country have reached out to ask if she thinks they can undertake similar efforts. Yes, she tells them. Use the playbook we have forged. She confesses she would love to see other communities identify all the people buried in their paupers' graves and, hopefully, close hundreds if not thousands of cold case murders. Help the families heal, she implores them. Make them people again by giving them back their names.

As the Detroit digging winds down, Leslie hears from the Philadelphia Police Department (PPD), asking if her FBI team can help with a smaller but similar effort in the City of Brotherly Love. It seems they know about a child, around two or four years of age, who was buried without a name in 1962. Another infant boy was buried in 1983. Three men and three women were buried between 1972 and 1984. All are cold case homicides. The eight victims were unidentified when buried in a small field in the northeast party of the city.

She has the playbook now and is sharing it willingly with PPD and other departments that are asking for assistance. Together with PPD, they determine the bodies are buried in a long-abandoned city cemetery. Leslie joins homicide Lt. Thomas Walsh and his team, explaining her process of identifying the locations, who is needed on scene, what to expect during the dig, and how long it will take to possibly get back DNA results.

She's excited, and Lt. Walsh is happy to discuss the effort with the press. They've been working on accomplishing this for three years, he tells the press. It's so important to the families.

That's what keeps the team going back in Detroit. After five years of digging, Leslie, Lori, Shannon and others see all the cold case murder files and missing people files differently. They dig into the files in an Operation UNITED-style investigation, and are beginning to match unidentified people with missing, all before anyone is buried. All the success, no digging required, Leslie says.

While Shannon focuses on the investigative work, Leslie continues to fight for testing, nudging to get the DNA results out of the overworked personnel at the FBI Laboratory in Quantico, Virginia. As positive DNA matches come in, Shannon and Lori stay connected, looking for clues in NamUS and other databases.

For five years, it has been a numbers game. The initial search for 206 bodies—not counting the ones they had to dig up to find the right person—resulted in recovered bones for 220 cases. The 57 or so different agencies—drawn from law enforcement, the scientific community, universities, and public and private organizations — that worked thousands of hours. Tens of thousands of federal and state tax dollars have been spent each year. Days have passed marking birthdays, marriages, deaths, babies, new homes, and graduations.

And though it's been a long time, it likely will take another five years or so to even submit all the bone fragments for DNA analysis to the FBI laboratory, unless things change. The lab has agreed to take five per month, prompting Leslie to text a friend, "I got them to help but because I have so many samples, they put me on a 5-body parts a month restriction. Each month I select my 5 favorite parts to send in for testing. I still have 50 parts to send in. The digs may be over, but it will take years to get all the parts through the doors of the lab for testing."

For Leslie, her childhood fascination of finding people and telling their stories did not get her to any Egyptian digs. With her work keeping her around her adopted home of Detroit, that old longing to be an archeologist is perhaps satisfied with the impact she is seeing up close. Halfway through the digs, she chose to become a certified Investigative Genealogist for the FBI for the sole purpose of solving Operation UNITED cases that came back negative in the CODIS system.

"Now I get to personally find the names of our forgotten people," she says, almost in awe of the opportunity. "That is truly an honor for me."

By the end of 2024, the effort yielded 26 positive identifications, a 12% solve rate with more still to come. It is at that moment—when a hit comes back—that the idea anyone is just a number disappears, and humanity returns.

One of the first DNA hits successfully returned the name Kareem Jabbor Laws to this world. Kareem's relatives discovered him missing, but didn't know for 15 years he was a number in a box buried six feet underground. Born in Detroit in 1972, he disappeared in 2005. His family knew he wasn't someone who just skipped town, as police might have thought. They suspected foul play.

Kareem's family had been looking for him through every channel they could find. They listed him as an endangered missing person right from the start. They posted pictures of the 32-year-old Black man with a Playboy bunny tattooed on the left side of his upper chest. His left ear was pierced. In fact, Kareem is still listed as a missing person on at least one of the websites of the many profit and not-for-profit organizations trying to help families, including one called The Charley Project. This site identifies Kareem and offers two photos, including one showing his brown hazel eyes hidden behind rose-colored glasses, and black hair covered with a cream-colored beret. The notes indicate Kareem "disappeared after a house fire and has never been heard from again."

This is the nightmare families can't wake up from. Families live in a void, knowing nothing about the fate of their relatives. Meanwhile, law enforcement has moved on to handle more pressing matters. For the Laws, they collectively wondered, checked sites, and listed his vital information wherever they could, but no leads ever emerged. Then, 15 years later, a brother, Karone, is called to Shannon's office to hear the news. Kareem had been killed, then burned, she explained to the family. She explained that his brother's murdered remains were found behind a garage the same year he went missing, discovered near the current Third Hope Baptist Church at Appoline Street and Plymouth Road.

"They found the body behind a garage. He'd been decomposing for three months," the brother Karone Law told a Detroit Channel 2 reporter. "They let us know that he had been there for years. That was good, in a sense, because we believed he was out there somewhere."

Before the wider availability of the Internet, families had to rely on law enforcement to look through their records. Families did not have access to details in police reports, such as interviews with potential suspects, neighbors, and witnesses. Those records, whether the FBI's or from state or local law enforcement's, are filled primarily with information on people arrested, convicted, or who had witnessed a crime. DNA would be available only for some, and then only consistently for investigations initiated in the past few decades.

The dearth of resources early on has shifted to an abundance of Internet opportunities for those looking for the long missing—whether runaways or murder victims—such as GoFundMe campaigns, social media sites, and more. Every year, the names of the missing are added to databases and websites of both for-profit and not-for-profit sites, encouraging the crowdsourcing of information. But the longevity, accuracy, and management of each site is not audited.

The Charley Project, one place where Kareen Law was listed, began as the Missing Persons Cold Case Network (MPCCN) founded in 2001 by Jennifer Marra. Marra also founded The Doe Network, a not-for-profit that highlights missing persons and has a team of volunteers providing guidance for families. Challenges in keeping these sites viable aren't just investigative or forensic. Marra, for example, resigned from the MPCCN and turned control over to Meaghan Good in December 2003. She ran the network until March 2004, when it was hacked and had to be taken offline. This led them to found The Charley Project in October 2004, ingesting into it much of the content of the former MPCCN. All the time, families of the missing are adding their loved one's information to any site they can find.

Early on, Shannon and Leslie set expectations for themselves and their teams. Their priority was to exhume bones that DNA could be drawn from. With a DNA profile, they would forever create a possibility of positively identifying the person in the grave they had re-interred. If they can't find the DNA match, maybe interested family sleuths can do it on their own. Identification is just the beginning. Plenty of steps lie between knowing someone was murdered, identifying them, developing suspects, gaining support from a prosecutor's office, criminally charging someone, and then either obtaining a guilty plea or holding a trial that may or may not result in a conviction.

Now that the digging is done and the DNA matches are beginning to trickle in, Shannon knows she needs to dig deeper and listen to the victims in her investigative files to try to solve each cold case murder file. Shannon and Lori reconnect as each new DNA match is made, looking for clues in NamUs and other databases. But Shannon is as practical as her daily, tightly tied ponytail. For these unknown murder victims, her priority has always been to identify victims, if possible, notify family, and close the cases for good. Pushing each case to the prosecution of a murder is another kettle of fish and an impractical gauge of success.

DNA results open doors and shed light on how complicated and challenging these cases can be for Shannon. Her cop reality is different than that of family members. She understands she may eventually identify the murderer, but the killer may still get away with it.

Since there is no margin of error in DNA matching, these matches are certainties. Some murder victims she identified through DNA turn out to match a family member and/or family members in prison. This is discovered when she finds a DNA match in the National DNA Index System (NDIS), the system where DNA involving criminal cases is stored within CODIS.

The reality is that these are not fictionalized murder mystery stories where everyone is categorized as either a good person or a bad person. Sometimes she can see that a family member may have been involved in the murder. Incarcerated family members are not likely to want to confess to killing their mother or brother. And no one wants to add more time to their existing prison sentences.

If a DNA match is from an inmate or former inmate, finding that person, their family, and those who knew someone who was murdered 30 or 40 years ago is still a challenge. DNA matches that come back to onetime prisoners who are now deceased can lead to a dead end. These are the messy and frustrating parts of investigations, yet they may still provide that relief of identification to family members.

No amount of work by police can overcome a missing link, however. Though the cemetery bones may yield a DNA profile, it still must be matched with known DNA. If a DNA match is not already in a database, the only hope is that a family member, even a distant relative, chooses to provide a DNA sample to look for a potential match. They can walk into a police station and provide a cheek swab, or they can order their own DNA results and upload that information into one of the databases. So many may not realize they are the best link to help solve both the case of a missing family member, and a murder they may have known nothing about.

If there are no living family members readily identifiable, there may be no way to match the DNA unless more distant relatives happen to hear and give DNA. Still, Shannon hopes items the team found buried with the murdered victim may give her new investigative leads. It might be medical implants that can now be traced, or dental oddities, or identifiable clothing. All the while, she persists in her daily assignments, knowing that the families offer the best hope.

She gets annoyed when she must explain that.

"I didn't find Anita," Shannon said gruffly to a podcast host. She is talking to Tonya Mosley, Anita Wiley's half-sister, who is now a celebrated and award-winning broadcaster. Tonya also is Antonio Wiley's aunt; someone he met for the first time when they were both adults. Three years after the DNA connection was made during Operation UNITED, Antonio sat down with Tonya to discuss his mom and explore their mutual lost family member.

A native of Detroit, Tonya is co-host, with Terry Gross, of National Public Radio's *Fresh Air* show. Her honors include an Emmy Award for her 2016 televised documentary, Beyond Ferguson, and a coveted national Edward R. Murrow award for her public radio series, Black in Seattle.

The honors are irrelevant to family needs. The story she wants to tell is about her nephew. As her podcast is recorded and airs, her comments reflect that she is often learning about the life of her previously unknown, but lost half-sister, Anita, and her nephew, Antonio. Tonya uses her best skills as a broadcaster to coax an interview out of Shannon and deflect her demeanor.

"I didn't find Anita," Shannon repeats. "I want to make that very clear. Antonio never stopped looking, and he did everything that he could do on his side. And because of his determination, he is the reason that Anita is now not in an unmarked gravesite. She is not now known as 'unknown woman 1987,' she has a name."

The emphatic nature of Shannon's tone likely prompted Tonya to title her 2024 podcast, She Has A Name. In his whispered and measured tone throughout the podcast, Antonio has found a way to tell not only his mom's story but his own story. This is his story, too, something sometimes forgotten when true crime enthusiasts focus on the criminal and whether a murderer is caught and sent to jail.

CHAPTER 25

Anita's Story

The story of her murder and Antonio begins long before, along with the family and friends who surrounded the murdered mother.

Anita was only 14 when Antonio was born on November 9, 1975. A child herself, she was now a mother. To many, she was one of those "throwaway people," half-sister Tonya says with disgust. Tonya was born five years after Anita, to a different mother.

In her short life, Anita endured and persevered through more than most do in a lifetime. Anita's mother, Caroline, was 16 when Anita was born, and two girls and a boy followed in succession. Their father had moved on to a new wife and a new life. He did that a lot. Antonio's arrival made a half dozen in the home, but only for a few years. When Anita's mother died, when she was 17, it changed their world.

A minor herself, Anita was responsible for her child and three siblings. She turned to dealing drugs to meet the family expenses.

Anita's sister, Val, was a few years younger. With loving notes of admiration for her sister, she shared some of the details with Tonya. "Neet," as they called their older sister, was industrious. She was keeping them fed. At times, she had all of them helping count cash and package drugs. She was keeping the house together. But Anita's move towards using drugs sent her on a path to self destruction.

Though family members recalled she had a nice boyfriend at one point, she also had the attention of someone else who did not treat her well. She was feisty, Val said. But her time in the 1970s and 1980s saw unprecedented struggles for Detroiters trying to scrape out a living and care for their families. At the time, the Department of Justice called Detroit the most dangerous city in America, and it earned the unwelcome title of Murder Capital of America after 714 people were killed in 1974, a sharp contrast to 252 by 2023.

Thousands of buildings had burned during the 1967 riots, displacing more Black residents, and prompting further White abandonment of the city. Dueling drug dealers made life dangerous for everybody there. All the street rules were changing about who could deal where and the hierarchy of dealing, Tonya learned from her newly acquainted family members. Anita also began carrying a gun.

As Antonio entered school, Anita was convicted in two drug cases but sentenced to probation, allowing her to keep Antonio home with her. Detroit had changed, become more dangerous, and safer territory lured her south to Ohio, sometimes to where Antonio's grandparents, Leo and Linda, lived. But as Antonio's age slipped into double digits, the physical abuse from Anita's boyfriend was unmistakable. Antonio stayed many nights at his grandparents while Anita was away. At times, she would show up with black eyes and bruises all over her body, Val told Tonya on the podcast. When Antonio was 11 or 12, Anita came home with a boot print on her chest.

While they occasionally stayed together at his grandparents, inevitably she would call for her boyfriend to come and get her, Val said, leaving Antonio for days at a time. He recalled to his Aunt Tonya that the whole situation eventually resulted in an explosion of frustration for his grandmother, who told Anita she had to either stop selling drugs, or leave, and take Antonio with her. Anita was 28 years old and no one could have known the fatal storm that would follow.

It was 1986 when they left. He wasn't asked about his preferences. He just recalled they moved for a couple of weeks to a homeless shelter in Detroit. It was embarrassing, he explained, because he had to take the bus to middle school every day, often in the same unwashed clothes. But two weeks later, she secured a small apartment for the two of them on the west side. It could have been a new chance, but she had habits and friends that did not change.

Most days, Antonio said, he would come home to an empty apartment, find something to eat, do his homework, and continue trying to learn how to navigate life. From time to time, on the days she was gone, Anita would call the house landline telephone later in the afternoon to check on him, but only speak briefly. She wanted to be sure he was home from school.

She never said where she was or when she would be home. He knew she was struggling with drug use. He had seen the bruises too and managed the familiar pattern of her disappearing and then returning. Then, one sunny day in 1987, Antonio asked his mom if he could spend the night at his cousin's house. She was in a good mood, so he knew he could ask.

She just had a moment to hug him, to say she loved him and to plant a kiss goodbye before he was out the door of their apartment.

"Remember," she told him, "We all we got."

He couldn't have known it was the last time. No one could have known. Coming home to an empty house the next morning, he waited. Hours turned into days and days turned into months. He took care of himself, selling what he could and believing that any moment his mom would return as she always had.

He never told his teachers that his mom was missing. They could tell something was wrong, he said. They even accused him of using drugs, which he was not. Antonio waited. His 15th birthday came and went. After that, in the recesses of his mind, he knew then she would not return.

Though it had not rung for a while, the house phone eventually was disconnected for failure to pay the bill. It was a crushing blow to Antonio, feeling he had lost the only way he had every been sure his mom could find him. Out of ideas, he walked to a payphone at Chicago Boulevard and Dexter Avenue. There were houses and businesses in the area then, not the endless vacant and abandoned lots that line the streets now looking up at a big brick Salvation Army building that still stands. Where 25 houses lined the streets in a block then, only four or five remain. Nothing from his past there seemed to survive except the pavement and his pain.

His dad was working as a tool and die setter for Ford at the time. Remarried and making a new life for himself, his dad's new family didn't know what he had been dealing with. They took him in. He recalls with affection how he was out walking one day with his father's wife and stopped in front of a church. Suddenly, he was overwhelmed with emotion and began to cry for the first time he could recall in his life. The tough façade crumbed away. She told him everything would be OK.

A year later, he moved to Cleveland to live with family there. Val, Anita's stepsister, said she was the one who filled out the missing person report. Now 16, Antonio thought about how he could finish school and make some money. His mother had taught him how to count, sort, and store large amounts of cash, he told his aunt on the podcast, so he thought holding the drug dealer's stash was a low risk, high value proposition.

"Two and a half million at five percent compound interest," he said, as if he was talking about the favorable rate he could get at his credit union. "Mom told me God bless the child who has his own. She said, 'You gotta take care of yourself.'"

But his mom didn't teach him how to successfully skirt the law. By the time he was 20 and already a father, he was sentenced to 15 years in prison on drug charges. Typical of state charges, he served six years. But Antonio had been industrious his whole life, and jail wasn't going to change that. While in prison, he earned his general education degree, helping him get his first legitimate full-time job when he was released. He went on to earn a bachelor's degree in business administration from Central Michigan University.

Soon he had a new life in Detroit, a good job, and a growing family. But Detroit is a big little town and what happened to Anita Wiley was never far away from his thoughts. He named his daughter Anita. He drove the streets he once spent time on with his mom: Joy Road, Livernois, West Davison, and Lawton. He remembered meeting with the FBI at one point, seeing if they could help. He recalled they were "dismissive."

His girlfriend's mother had heard about the Missing in Michigan program where the Michigan State Police were trying to collect cheek swabs to look for DNA matches. That's why he visited the Missing in Michigan tent that spring day in 2016, meeting Shannon for the first time.

For Antonio, that was just one more effort, but then the call came. He recalled that it was a palindrome day when Shannon called on February 2, 2020. Come to the police station, she said.

It was joy and pain, he recalled in a conversation with his aunt on the podcast. At police headquarters, he was characteristically stoic until he stepped into the elevator to leave. As the doors closed, "I melted," he said. "I haven't cried since I was a kid, but I definitely cried that day." It was the second time in his life.

The years had given Antonio breathing room to understand what happened to his mom. As a child, he felt alone in his struggle. But as an adult, he believes she is a symbol for more complex problems and the idea that some lives are expendable in society. The Freedom of Information file detailing the discovery of Anita Wiley's body is minimal.

Firefighters found the badly burned torso of a woman who would be identified 33 years later as Anita Wiley. Detectives determined she had been strangled to death, most likely before she was brought to the house.

Still, every fact is precious to Antonio. The reports detail that a dog barking near 17719 Wanda Street at 4:00 a.m. awakened nearby residents. It was Wednesday, November 11, 1987, just two days after Antonio's 15th birthday. Gilbert Howard and Dixi Collins explained to firefighters that it was their dog barking, but they saw nothing. Another neighbor, Phyllis Edwards, called 911 after seeing bright orange flames shooting from the vacant house. She reported seeing a male figure striking a match and throwing a lit object down before the house erupted in flames.

Fire investigators noted that burn marks indicated gasoline had been intentionally poured on the first floor and on the body of the woman. It was a "clear case of arson," the report said.

At the time, DPD's police reports offered five standard boxes officers could check under the heading: Were the Following Solvable Factors Present in this Incident? Officers had marked the "no" box for each: arrests, descriptions of perpetrators, witnesses, vehicle numbers, physical evidence. The report was submitted by 1:20 p.m. the next afternoon. There were no leads to follow. Police moved on.

When they first spoke, and Antonio learned his mother had been found, he said it transported him back to his childhood. Shannon was the one who later told Antonio that his mom was seven or eight months pregnant when she was killed. Anita had been gone for months by then. But his mother had never missed his birthday. He remembered that 15th birthday in 1987 and how he knew things might never be the same.

"It's something I've thought about my whole adult life," Antonio tells his aunt Tonya in her podcast. "It's just something as heinous as you can imagine. It's really a nightmare and you can't wake up no matter how hard you try."

When Shannon first took Antonio's DNA, she had scoured through the files to see if there was a match of an unidentified murder victim found around his neighborhood or another. Always overly critical of herself, she faults her failure to take what she learned from Antonio and then match it to Anita's file among the hundreds in the warehouse. She had looked at several missing and unidentified people around the time of Anita's disappearance. But Anita disappeared seven or eight months before she was killed, so Shannon was looking for an unidentified dead person found in spring 1987, when Anita's body was found and buried in the late fall. Little about the file that eventually came to be associated with Anita would have likely jumped out to any investigator.

Though Anita was 29 when she was killed, detectives had estimated the age of the Wanda Street victim as a woman possibly between 15 and 20 years old. Anita was just over five feet tall. For the podcast, Tonya's team did their own investigating, telling Antonio they discovered a newspaper story from around that time of a teenager found burned in a building. It could have been her stepsister, Tonya says, but she doesn't know for sure. Still, Shannon blames herself for not giving Antonio back his mother three or four years earlier.

Through it all a singular question remained, who killed Anita Wiley?

"We don't have any DNA evidence that would help connect things," Shannon told Tonya. "We don't have any video or cell phone records of who she was talking to or possibly hanging out with."

Family members have developed four theories they share, but in their hearts, the facts point to the final theory. She could have left on her own to start a new life. She was involved with someone else and managing a problem with drugs. Or she might have been the victim of a serial killer who was stalking the city around that time, though that killer primarily attacked sex workers, and no evidence points to any connection to the case. A fourth theory is that a rival drug dealer simply killed Anita. But again, no clues point to that.

"The police department can't go on feelings," Shannon tells Tonya.

Most victims of homicide know their killer and most acts of violence are not random. Antonio knows his mother was strangled and pregnant when she died. The Shelter for Abused Women and Children reports that one in four women will experience intimate partner violence in their lifetime, and of those, up to 68 percent will suffer near-fatal strangulation at the hands of their partner. The Wings Program in Chicago reports the number one cause of death among pregnant women in the United States is homicide by an intimate partner.

The most likely scenario? Everyone knew Anita was being beaten by the person she was seeing. Her money was tight. Her recreational drug use was becoming a habit.

It was Leroy Lyons who had left a boot mark on her chest and beat her so badly that she fled with Antonio to her little sister Val's house in Cleveland. The relationship hadn't started out violently. Leroy and Anita met around 1982 after he served time for robbing a bank, Tonya learned. They were selling drugs and romance likely sparked at that time. It was a bit frustrating to some in the family. Antonio's memories are fuzzy, but other family told Tonya they knew Anita was living with a man named James at the time, a person that Antonio viewed as a stepfather. As James faded from the scene, Leroy spent more time at their place. They went to his place too, a house that had locks, bars, and doors that could only be opened from the outside.

Though Anita fled to the safety of Val and her husband Frank's house, she would sometimes call Leroy to come and get her to go back to Detroit. They returned together, staying at the shelter and then the apartment. What led to her being found in the abandoned, burned down house in 1987 may never be fully explained. The fire and police reports show that neighbors saw two men walking in and out of the abandoned Wanda Street house for a week before it burned. Some neighbors thought the men were taking salvage out of the house. But another neighbor reported seeing a man in the window strike a match and drop it to the ground. The flames followed. Tonya wanted to know more, but she discovered the neighbors have since passed on.

Their only lead is Leroy Lyons himself. His very public life story shows the violence that enveloped his world; violence directed towards those he might have pretended he loved.

Leroy was a person of interest, Shannon stresses, not a suspect. But Val is sure it was Leroy, and many in her family think so too.

Law enforcement learned that Leroy and his brother, Preston Lyons, murdered two of their own family members in November 1987, just days after Anita was strangled and burned nearly beyond recognition. In the brothers' trial for the double murder, prosecutors noted that Preston was the enforcer for his drug dealing brother, Leroy.

Their victims? Leroy's niece, Antoinette Bates, and her boyfriend, Christopher Clark. They are accused of trying to steal some of Leroy's money. Clark's body was found in the trunk of Lyon's father's car when firefighters responded to a call about a burning car. Bates' body was never recovered.

In the few years after the murders of Anita, Christopher, and Antionette—but before his murder trial sent him to prison for two concurrent life sentences—Leroy and his wife were charged with criminal negligence in connection with the deadliest house fire to ever occur in Detroit. Newspapers as far away as Los Angeles wrote about the couple charged and later acquitted after seven children, all under the age of nine, burned to death when they were left alone in a building secured with security bars and locks that could only be opened from the outside.

It's one of the many stories Antonio, Val, and others recall in their theory that Leroy is to blame. Antonio believes the circumstances of his mother's death point to an intimate relationship gone badly.

"This isn't a 'I love you and can't live without you' crime," Antonio told his Aunt Tonya on one gripping episode of her podcast. "This is a jealous rage. This is calculated. This is murder."

Leroy is alive and in jail for life for the double murder, Tonya learns. Still, law enforcement and family alike recognize that a serial domestic abuser has little incentive to confess to Anita's brutal death by strangulation.

The podcast seems a healing process for both Antonio and his Aunt Tonya. They laugh a lot, and she tears up some, appearing to realize they are both grieving for Anita anew. Tonya gave him a reason to share his story, a story he hadn't even told his five children. For years, he said, he glossed over and used generalizations to deflect questions about his mother. She died of cancer; he recalled telling one child. He couldn't find the words. Now he had permission to tell the story at his own pace, in his own space.

But none of that is closure, he said, a word that people often use. We've all heard bystanders use various descriptions to characterize how those left behind should feel and what they might want. What does healing look like? Do you want justice? They are asked. Do you feel closure? Antonio has found his peace, but closure is an illusion.

"In God's eyes, we already got it," he says calmly.

To him, there is no beginning or end to the story of Anita and Antonio. He sees the life they had and the life he continues to live. He was raised to be civilized, he explains, and his cautious and careful management of his story and his world has allowed him to thrive.

He returned to United Memorial Gardens not too long after he first placed flowers on his mother's grave by the fence near the Crimson Norway Maple. Now it was time to introduce his five kids to their grandmother, Anita Wiley. He shared not only the details of her life but also details of his own life that had been locked away for 33 years.

Now, they celebrate her homegoing.

On a bright Sunday in March, Uncle Frank and Aunt Val gathered with Antonio and his family. Everyone looked down at the stone: Anita A. Wiley, August 3, 1958 - November 11, 1987. Loving mother. Truly missed."

Uncle Frank officiated. Antonio recalls Anita as a fashionista and stylish mother who had an eye for interior design. She was a social butterfly who loved life, he said. Everyone seemed to love her and miss her. So many relied on her in life, and she did not let them down.

Even in death, voices cannot be silenced. Tonya recalls feeling as if Anita was speaking through her nephew, letting them all know she is at rest now that she has been found.

Anita's last diary entries were written at the end of March 1987, Antonio says, when she was probably four months pregnant. They reflect the hopes, dreams, and desires we all have to be loved, and to conquer our demons. "Cocaine, fighting to quit." "Sometimes it's hard." "To me, like cocaine, you are a sign of my weakness."

Anita struggled without a support system so many have. Her lifestyle consumed her as she held on for the ride and dedicated her life to taking care of her family

"My heart cries," Antonio whispers.

His one regret, he tells his Aunt Tonya: "I wish I could have saved her."

But just like he knows his mother didn't abandon him, he'll never abandon his mom. They'll be back on August 3, if not before. That's Anita's birthday.

CHAPTER 26

The Cheese Stands Alone

As intense as the planning for the digs has been, the DPD never created a parallel publicity campaign to find DNA matches in the community. There was one time when the DPD's media office released a one-paragraph announcement, but it was laden with law enforcement language. Members of the media ignored it.

Today, the Detroit Police Department and its partners in law-enforcement launched Operation UNITED. (Unknown Names Identified Through Exhumation and DNA) aimed at utilizing new technologies to identify unknown victims. With the advancement of technology and DNA, this operation will focus on victims of homicides dating back to 1959 that currently do not have DNA on file. Over the next few months, Detroit police and its partners will exhume unidentified homicide remains for the collection of DNA in efforts to identify the victims. The collection of the DNA will be sent to the National Missing and Unidentified Person System (NAMUS), and processed at their Human Identification Lab. Once in the lab it will be uploaded into the Combined DNA Index System (CODIS), as well as the FBI's National DNA Index System (NDIS) to be searched against all appropriate indexes for potential associations. Detroit is asking families of loved ones to come forward and submit DNA to help identify the victims. Special acknowledgment to Detroit Police Department PIO partners who are assisting in this operation: Wayne County Prosecutor's office, Detroit Building Authority Department of Public Works, the FBI, Michigan State Police, National Missing and Unidentified Persons System, University of North Texas Center for Human Identification and Crime Stoppers of Michigan.

Leading the silence is Shannon, who generally rejects publicity and anything that might require her to speak in public. She has done only a few interviews in a half-dozen years; contributions obtained only by the most persistent reporters.

Nearly a decade after the idea started brewing in Shannon's mind, there is still little being done to advertise to the public the critical need for families who believe they may have a long-lost, missing relative to come forward to provide DNA for potential matches.

Maybe it's because Shannon knows she'll need to talk more. Maybe it's because she worries the public won't turn out because family members have moved on or died or fear any contact with the police is bad contact. Maybe it's because complicit family members never wanted the murder of an adult, or worse a baby, solved. Maybe many Detroiters would rather forget this darker part of their history.

Operation UNITED was premised, in part, on a rejection of the stereotype that all victims are somehow perfect people struck down in the prime of their life. Reality is messier. Those who have spent five years giving up all their free time have focused repeatedly on a person's worth. Having no name shouldn't make a person less worthy to mourn. It's a widespread thought voiced by those who worked the digs.

Maybe Shannon believes deep down that no one is really conversing with these murder victims except for her and Leslie. Perhaps murder victims whisper to them their disbelief than they have been forgotten. And, neither Shannon nor Leslie know how to tell them for certain that that is not true.

Cold case homicide and missing person cases can only be solved if the families want them solved. Law enforcement can't lead the way, Shannon says, families must. It's a family's moxie that brought Anita and Antonio Wiley back together.

Antonio likely will never return to the DPD headquarters building. He doesn't need to talk to Shannon again. His life has taken a permanent turn for the better.

Sarah Krebs has moved on to find others still missing in Michigan. Dr. Jaymelee Kim at Wayne State University and Dr. Carolyn Isaac at Michigan State University are still in the fight. LaDonna Logan left the Wayne County prosecutor's office to become a Michigan assistant attorney general, leading their Hate Crimes and Domestic Terrorism Unit.

Dr. Jane (Wankmiller) Harris and her team are still training and researching at Northern Michigan University's FROST Center, as are Giovanna Vidoli, Joanne Devlin, Dawnie Steadman, Lee Meadows Jantz, and Mary Davis, who is running the Forensic Anthropology Center Body Farm at the University of Tennessee.

The last year of the digs, Leslie's mom became more fragile, and then died. The person who urged her to collect the summer internship application that summer in Washington, D.C. Like Shannon's loss of her father, Leslie's loss was so hard. Did her mom know how their actions impacted the lives of so many others?

That dream of becoming a profiler. "It's still there," she says. "But I think I'm not an archeologist because I crave the back story. Why are these people killing? Who are they choosing—the victimology that they're choosing? And I just have this inherent calling to go get the victims. Wherever you are, I wanna go get you."

It's the drive that keeps her pushing her forensic team from one investigation to another. Saving one more life, or perhaps just explaining one more life.

Jodi completed her tour of duty molding tomorrow's scientists at Madonna University and returned to Canada. She knows the impact of giving someone back their identity.

"This is not about judging a person's condition at the time of their death," she says. "This is about the human factor, the network. There was this little boy whose mother went missing, and he never knew what happened to her," she notes. "Did his mother not want him? Did his mother just run away because she didn't love him? That sense of abandonment is incredible. And we were able to reconnect that boy with his mother, and he was able to find out when she was buried and he found out that she didn't run away, she had been murdered. You can't pay for that.

"We are all connected. It's about a little boy whose life was changed when he found out that his mother did not abandon him. That's going to make him a better man. It's going to make him a better father. It's gonna make him probably a better member of his community."

People who lose track of someone lose part of their themselves, she says, reflecting on her own life.

"There are still people looking for those people," Jodi says. "People have a little piece of their heart knowing potentially, one day, that person might walk through the door. So, until there is closure, and we can say, 'Yes, we know where your person is, that person will forever, be in a piece of their heart, till the day they die, waiting for them to walk through the door."

Pulled by hundreds of heart strings, Shannon remains the lone key to finish the work. She knows the public's interest in solving these murders is fleeting. Solving 200 or so murders one at a time is the only way they can be worked. Every so often, they get word of another DNA profile match. They have a few dozen already. No victim is forgotten to Leslie and Shannon.

They work apart more now, with few reasons to connect during the busy days. But both are still talking with the victims so few can hear. Shannon knows her role. Each DNA identification allow investigators to begin with where the victim lived and worked. What kind of relationship did they have with family members? What can she discover about where they were living and whether they were living risky or vulnerable lifestyles? Were they, unfortunately, in the wrong place at the wrong time?

Each person was given a name at birth, but became a number when they were murdered. A growing number have become people again thanks to a seismic effort led by dedicated women who knew how and were willing to talk to the dead. Even as you read these words, scientists, including inside the massive FBI Laboratory at Quantico, Virginia, are working to extract DNA from the bones Leslie and Shannon have provided.

Shannon plans to spend the rest of her career truly solving murders and closing files, one file jacket at a time. She can't shelve them as if they were misaddressed letters being tossed into the dead letter box at the post office.

Huddled over her desk in her tucked away corner, Shannon remains surrounded by boxes and papers tacked up on her walls. Her desk is just as messy as it was a decade ago, long before the cemetery lawsuits, the pandemic, funding battles, equipment failures, mistaken casket raisings, battles with her supervisors, and undesired media attention.

She will never quite be alone again as each new match provides a name for each murder victim. Now, many have names, whether it be Gerald, Susan, or Roger. There are still faces looking back at her from those walls and she sometimes is heard talking to them.

If too many victims are speaking at the same time, she won't be overwhelmed. Leslie will know and will call.

"The morning my mom died," Leslie recalls, "Shannon called me. She said she had a feeling something was wrong. We're just always connected."

Occasionally, Shannon takes in the slowly dwindling number of cold case files and those faces and reports tacked on the cloth walls that still bear the notes, *Who Am I?* and *Where Am I?*

Shannon intends to find out.Nequi seni dellace archill entempo rehenih iciendis eatas qui blandes si suntotate eicae dusda eosam, comnimo luptaqui quam, que sendige nissinu llatum aces voluptatisto blaborporrum con re de con eos eume doluptus adit ipsam ium quaessi cus elias ese lat ut ad qui ullectia vel illabor simusandam, om-

LETTER FROM THE AUTHOR

Dear Readers,

Thank you for allowing me to share the story of these remarkable women through my book, *Women Who Talk to the Dead.* Many women I interviewed for this book, including friends I spoke to while I was writing, shared their detailed and sometimes surreal experiences of feeling the presence of the dead. Whether called intuition or something else, it's clear these women often hear and feel what the men around them may not.

In the five-year journey to bring this story to life, I watched a cadre of women do what no one even tried to accomplish in the 60 years before–name these murder victims. Even today, these women continue to pursue the identities of more than 200 murder victims, connect them with surviving families, and solve their murders.

Please help me share their story by writing a short review on **Amazon** and **Goodreads**—your insights help others discover the book. Follow me to stay informed about new releases and connect with me on social media for sneak peeks, thoughtful analysis, and updates.

Please consider joining my email list and visit my website to access my blog and resource library. All of this and more is accessible by scanning the QR code.

Thank you again and remember, **Kindness is Free**.

Happy Reading,
Katherine Schweit

OTHER WORKS

In *Stop the Killing*, mass shooting expert Katherine Schweit, creator of the FBI's Active Shooter Program, provides an insider's look at what works—and what doesn't—when it comes to stopping mass shootings.

This book cuts through confusion, demystifying facts while offering real-life lessons from tragedies like Columbine, Sandy Hook, Virgina Tech, and Oxford.

You'll gain the knowledge and tools to take action and be part of the solution. Ready to replace fear with power? You can.

The Second Amendment now fuels one of America's most divisive debates over guns.

This easy-to-read, politics-free guide unpacks history, Supreme Court rulings, and key topics such as background checks, red flag laws, ghost guns, and mental health.

Packed with facts and practical solutions, it debunks misinformation and empowers you to take action.

Learn the facts. Explore solutions. Help end the violence.

A Study of 160 Active Shooter Incidents in the United States, 2000 – 2013, FBI

Handbook of Gun Violence,

Edited by Nicholas D. Thomson, contributor

“Safety isn't about the odds of it whether it will happen; safety is about being prepared if it does happen.”

-From *Stop the Killing: How to End the Mass Shooting Crisis* by Katherine Schweit

FINDING OUR WAY OUT OF

AMERICA'S GUN CULTURE

WATCH THE TEDx Talk

SCAN THE QR CODE

Imagine if we could retool the way we think about guns in America...

How are we going to change our culture? There is no perfect path or single solution...

... I invite you to think of ways to return to a culture where **guns are tools and not symbols of power and superiority.**

Printed in Dunstable, United Kingdom